SINGLE, READY & WAITING:

YOUR GUIDE TO COURTSHIP, A NEW PERSPECTIVE

SINGLE
READY &
WAITING

YOUR GUIDE TO COURTSHIP
A NEW PERSPECTIVE

TANIKA A. CHAMBERS

Belleville, Ontario, Canada

ISBN: 978-1-55452-913-1
LSI Edition: 978-1-55452-914-8

Cataloguing data available from Library and Archives Canada

To order additional copies, visit:
www.essencebookstore.com

For more information, please contact:
www.singlereadyandwaiting.com
tanika@singlereadyandwaiting.com

Guardian Books is an imprint of *Essence Publishing,* a Christian Book Publisher dedicated to furthering the work of Christ through the written word. For more information, contact:
20 Hanna Court, Belleville, Ontario, Canada K8P 5J2
Phone: 1-800-238-6376 • Fax: (613) 962-3055
Email: info@essence-publishing.com
Web site: www.essence-publishing.com

DEDICATION

To God first, as He is the one who continues to be my guide. I don't know who or where I would be if it had not been for Your love, grace and mercy. You are the reason I am alive today and You deserve all the glory.

To my wonderful husband, Robert Chambers (who was also my part-time content editor and producer of the SRW theme song "Stop, Wait, Go!"), thank you for your support and patience. God brought us together on purpose (for a purpose) and you make the principles shared in this book a practical reality. I love you and I thank God for all that you do.

To my sweet, loving mother, thank you for praying and supporting all that I do. Your smile and words of humour always brighten my day. I love you very much!

Dad, they say I am your twin. Thank you for showing me what ambition is and for having me read those Psalms in the morning before heading off to school. I love you and I am so thankful for that.

To my first editor, Veronica Chambers, how can I ever thank you. I am so blessed to have you as my mother-in-law. I love you and appreciate your labour of love.

To my second editor, Kerri-Ann Haye-Donawa of Conclusio Inc., thank you so much for making this book even better.

To my Pastor Orim Meikle and First Lady Judith Meikle, your support and spiritual covering means the world to me. Thank you and I love you both.

Family and friends, thank you for believing in me and praying for me when I needed it most. Your ongoing support means a lot to me.

And last but not least, to the Single, Ready and Waiting community, both near and far, this book is dedicated to you. By now everyone knows or has an idea of how to date, but only a very few know how to court and make it down the aisle. Be blessed by the information shared in this book, and know that "God Has A Master Plan With Your Name On It!"

CONTENTS

FOREWORD

Today more than ever, people long for connection. In an age marked by isolation and loneliness, we've come to realize that riches are best measured in relationships that offer belonging, acceptance, vulnerability, honesty, closeness, and commitment.

Between singleness and marriage lives the journey of courting. To make your road as smooth as possible you should maintain healthy self-control by setting boundaries. The author has captured your attention with honesty, vulnerability and transparency through her own personal struggle.

I met Tanika about five years ago and I strongly believe God directed our paths to meet at that time and place. She is a young woman who loves God with every fibre of her being and lives for the sole purpose of pleasing Him. Though she strayed from the will of God, He restored her with a message. I found her honesty and openness to be breathtaking and I believe her to be a woman of purpose who will impact her generation. This book is a must read!

Tanika has taken a step that many would be afraid to take; becoming transparent with her own wrong decisions and her journey back. If you have, or are still battling with waiting on the Lord for a mate, not taking matters into your own hands, tempted to settle for less than God's best, pressure to have sex outside of marriage, whatever the reason, here is a testimony that the blood of Jesus has not lost its power.

The author has given you her naked truth which can now empower you to make right decisions along your journey. I believe this book is a good guide towards courtship. *"For I know the plans I have for you, declares the Lord. Plans to prosper you and not to harm you, plans to give you hope and a future"* (Jeremiah 29:11 NIV).

My prayer is that those who are still in the struggle will now have the knowledge and empowerment to walk away single, saved, sanctified and waiting for God's best.

What a testimony!

Reverend Ruth-Yvonne Brown B.Th., MCC, OPC

PREFACE

Love is a wonderful thing and we all desire to meet that one person we want to spend the rest of our lives with. But, what if we're not really Single, Ready or willing to Wait for it? Then what? Well, in order to develop a strong marriage from the start there is a level of preparedness required.

Are you single, dating, or engaged and desire to get married one day? Well, the first step to getting there is to know…right now…where you are. You now have in your hands the right book at the right time to guide you through the stages of what it truly means to be single, ready and waiting. What do you consider to be a good road guide? Is it the way you will know what to expect up ahead? Or the way it leads you to your destination? Whatever the reason, one thing is for sure, road guides serve a very good purpose.

As your road guide towards courtship, let me tell you a bit about myself. Those who know me well say I have a sense of humour, I am driven, goal oriented with a bottom line personality, and I don't like to beat around the bush to get a point across. The way I write in this book will be the same.

Having spent eight long years in a relationship that was not the will of God for me, I've learned two important things about time: how to value and respect my time better and how to value and respect the time of others as well. Therefore, like a surgeon called into emergency, I will go in and out as fast and carefully as I can, however not without exposing a hidden wound or two.

Many times, people refrain from telling their friends and loved ones the truth about themselves or situation, fearing they would offend and lose their friendship for good. But the Word of God says: *"Faithful are the wounds of a friend; but the kisses of an enemy are deceitful"* (Proverbs 27:6). In life, we must learn to love and appreciate those that tell us what we often don't want to hear, but need to hear. Hearing the good, the bad and the ugly about ourselves, or a particular situation we might be involved in can help us to grow and mature into the men and women God has called us to be. By the time this surgery is over, you will get a clear understanding of what the difference between dating and courting is and how you can be prepared and guided towards experiencing your very own "sacred stage of courtship" and much more. May your heart be open and receptive to the principles shared, and consider applying them to your own life. These principles will be referred to as "Single Ready and Waiting (SRW) Signals."

Be informed! Be empowered! Be equipped! Be free!

INTRODUCTION

Whether you travel by bus or by car the question remains the same: do you always obey the traffic laws? Well, if we are honest with ourselves I'm sure that all of us at some time or another have disobeyed the law for a number of reasons. It could have been that we were running late, not paying close attention, the police were not around or we were distracted i.e. cell phone! No matter the reason, the law is still the law, and we are expected to be law abiding citizens. What happens when we are caught breaking the law? You said it: tickets, fines and even imprisonment. Have you ever been caught breaking the law? What did you do? Did you lie your way through it? Or confess?

Through experience I've learned that honesty is always the best policy. People have been forgiven plenty of speeding tickets because of their honesty alone.

So how does this apply to this book? *Single, Ready and Waiting* represents the traffic lights for a very good reason. Traffic lights have a great purpose and that is to bring order to our roads and more importantly bring us safely to our destination (if obeyed of course). They can be found at road intersections, pedestrian crossings, and other locations to control the flow of traffic. When a light stops working, a police officer is usually called to the scene to direct traffic. Or we somehow work it out amongst ourselves, which can be dangerous. In case you have forgotten, this is what a universal traffic light does:

✓Red Light Signal (STOP)—prohibits any traffic from proceeding.

✓Amber Light Signal (WAIT)—proceed with caution or prepare to stop.

✓Green Light Signal (GO)—allows traffic to proceed in the direction desired.

Like these traffic signals, the "SRW Signals" will help guide you safely towards a healthy courting relationship. But before I explain them, I want to be completely honest with you, not every courting relationship will make it to the altar. Being in a courting relationship with the wrong person is heading towards a collision and nothing more. In the next stop, you will find out about my own collision and how I could have lost it all, even my life.

Let's go!

SRW Signals

Get familiar with these "SRW Signals" they will be used throughout this book to bring awareness to the direction you should go.

SRW Signal #1—Seek godly counsel (WAIT)

SRW Signal #2—Knowing God's Word for yourself (WAIT)

SRW Signal #3—Wait for the spiritual release from God (WAIT)

SRW Signal #4—Equally yoked (GO) Not equally yoked (STOP)

SRW Signal #5—Being led by the flesh (STOP)

SRW Signal #6—Heading in the wrong direction (STOP)

SRW Signal #7—Follow the leading of the Holy Spirit (GO)

SRW Signal #8—Pray for clarity (WAIT)

SRW Signal #9—Heading in the right direction (GO)

SRW Signal #10—Take the nearest exit (GO)

To Courtship or Collision?

2005 was the worst year of my life and at times I still cannot believe that I survived to tell it, but I did. God sends us signals all the time about things we should or should not do, places we should or should not go, and people we should or should not enter into a courting relationship with. Whether we take heed to those signals or not is the question.

Have you ever had somewhere to go and were in a rush to get there? You happen to approach an amber light that has been amber for some time, and still decide to proceed? The result: you end up running a red light—endangering not only yourself but others too. So it can be with one's desire for marriage. Rather than following what I call the "HGPS" (Holy Ghost Protection Service), which is our most reliable guide, we ignore the signals He gives, and end up in relationships we are not meant to be in. The result: you end up wasting time, hurting others and yourself. As your road guide, I am not telling you something I haven't experienced first hand. I ignored the guiding signals and ended up spending eight years (a time that I could have spent living my life to the fullest as a single) in a relationship that came to a surprising halt.

What I Hope You Will Learn from My Story

- ✓The importance of entering a courting relationship at the right time
- ✓The importance of understanding God's Word
- ✓The importance of spiritual covering and not speaking against authority
- ✓The importance of knowing how sin takes you down a road you don't want to go
- ✓The importance of knowing that your decisions can steal, kill and destroy you
- ✓The importance of knowing that the curses for disobedience are real
- ✓The importance of obedience in a believer's life
- ✓The importance of knowing that God redeems and restores
- ✓The importance of being truly single
- ✓The importance of being truly ready
- ✓The importance of truly waiting

My Story

I share this story only for your learning and not to put anyone in a negative light. We learn from our mistakes and move on to making better decisions in the future. The names of the people in this story have been changed to protect their identity.

I met Peter in university at the age of 21. I was a new Christian when we met and he wasn't at the time (SRW Signal #4). I knew he had an interest in me but I kept him at bay because of the Christian factor. School came to an end and I was really struggling with the idea of going back home, especially after gaining so much independence being away. With so many of us finishing school at the same time, I knew that Windsor, Ontario, wouldn't have enough jobs to go around, so I went back home to the big city of Toronto, Canada.

Things were not going too well for my family at home. My dad had left and gone back to Jamaica and my mother had to handle things on her own. Without my dad in the picture I often felt like there were too many heads in the house, if you know what I mean. Usually my dad would have the last say and the arguments would be over. Being the only Christian child in my family at that time, I prayed for and invited my brothers and sisters to church often. At times, I wondered who was praying for me. Before Dad left he held prayer meetings in our basement. When my friends came over, it wasn't hard for them to tell that our basement was the prayer room in our house; my dad wrote "Prayer Room" everywhere. I couldn't go to our washing machine without coming across those words at least ten times. I laugh about it now, but it was in this "Prayer Room" that I cried and prayed for God's guidance and strength to live out my Christian walk. The "Prayer Room" wasn't the only place I prayed that prayer. After my water baptism in Detroit, Michigan at the Perfecting Church, I prayed that same prayer in my dorm. "Lord, I ask you for your guidance and strength, and that you will show me my purpose in life." A few days later I sensed a strong calling on my life for evangelism.

Job Search in Toronto

After sending out a few resumes, I decided to call my previous employer to see if there were any job openings. To my surprise there was an opening with my name on it! Back to the *Toronto Star* I went. Two years later, work began to feel like a drag. I lacked passion and purpose in my life and often thought "Certainly, there has got to be more to my life than this." Then I got a call from a friend of mine about a business he was involved in.

Business Opportunity

"You will have the opportunity of becoming financially free; and check this out, when you bring people to the yearly functions they can receive salvation too," he said. The excitement on his face while sharing grabbed my full attention. "Could this be what I have been looking for?" I thought to myself. "So, do you want to come out to a meeting?" he asked. "Sure, why not?" I said. I accompanied him to a meeting, signed up and got "fired up!" like the rest of them. After a few meetings, I began fantasizing about going to my mother's workplace and letting her know she wouldn't have to work another day in her life, with all the cash I would be making.

Time to Call Peter

"The best time to build your business is when there is a function" they would often say. So when the next function rolled around I prayed about who I could invite, Peter immediately came to mind. Knowing that he liked me, I struggled with the idea, so I prayed again. This time the Holy Spirit spoke very clearly: "Bring Peter to the function; I am going to save him there" (SRW Signal #7). I was excited and jumped up from being on my knees and gave Peter a call. Clearly, this function was much bigger than getting a new business partner. Though the function was only three days away, Peter considered my invitation and decided to attend. Off to Raleigh, North Carolina we went.

The Last Day of the Function

We entered the stadium, which was built to fit approximately 20,000 people, and took our seats. After a few short hours, the place was packed with excited business owners and their guests. Because it was a Sunday, they started off with prayer, then praise and worship before the heavy hitter speaker, Bill Blake, took the stage. I thought, if there was anyone that could get through to my friend Peter, it would definitely be Bill Blake. Having heard so much about him I felt as though I knew who he was.

When the praise and worship died down Bill Blake came on stage. He encouraged the business owners and then delivered the following words. "No matter how much money you make, without a personal relationship with Jesus Christ you are lost." I thought, 'Here comes the crucial moment.' I glanced over at Peter and saw that he was fast asleep. "Oh no you don't!" I said in a quiet voice. Then I immediately began to pray, reminding God about His word to save him at the function. Not a minute later, Peter sat up and opened his eyes. Bill Blake repeated "No matter how much money you make, without a personal relationship with Jesus Christ you are lost. If you're in this stadium and have not accepted Jesus Christ as your Saviour, you need to make your way down to this altar and accept Him today." Peter looked at me, got out of his seat and went down to the altar. I was ecstatic and began thanking God for His faithfulness. Then I heard, "Your job is done!" (SRW Signal #7). "My job is done?" What does that mean? (SRW Signal #8) I remember thinking.

A few weeks later, Peter and I began speaking on the phone more often. I told him he needed to get baptized and just a few months later, he did so at his grandmother's church. We became even closer friends after that. But the words "your job is done" (SRW Signal #7) kept ringing in my mind. I didn't give it much thought. (Now, however, I know it was a signal from the Holy Spirit trying to keep me from entering a relationship with Peter. By then, my emotions got the best of me and I neglected to pray and pay close attention to the guiding signals [SRW Signal #8]). Soon I really fell for Peter. Details were not important to us; the fact that we were both Christians now and could date was all we needed to know, right? (SRW Signal #6).

My First Visit

Being a naive young woman in my early twenties, I went along with Peter's idea to book a hotel room for me while I visited for the weekend (Peter didn't live in Canada). When I arrived at the bus terminal, Peter picked me up, brought me to the hotel to drop off my bags and took me out for dinner. We never got back to the hotel until after eleven. This is when Peter decided to stay with me for the night (SRW Signal #6). "Where are you going to sleep?" I asked.

"Nothing is going to happen," he replied. So he came into bed with me (SRW Signal #6).

"What are you doing Peter?" I asked in a soft but serious tone.

"Don't worry, I'm going to marry you," he said. The next thing I knew, he forced himself on me (SRW Signal #5).

That night I couldn't sleep. I kept replaying what happened over and over again in my mind. Because of my naiveté, I had put myself in a dangerous position. "Peter just allowed his flesh to get the best of him that night, that's all, it happens," I said to myself (SRW Signal #1). So I forgave him and moved on. I didn't tell a soul about what happened in that hotel room. I kept it a secret like so many women do (SRW Signal #1). After this, our relationship was never the same. We thought we were heading towards courtship but we were really headed towards a collision.

Over the next year, our relationship was on-again, off-again. Even with my doubts, and Peter's frustration, we still really wanted it to work. We invested so much time and energy to just throw it all away (SRW Signal #5). When we got back together again for the fourth time, I decided that my pastor needed to finally know about our relationship (SRW Signal #1, #9). My church at the time was very traditional, and they did things a certain way; a way that I grew to respect and admire a lot. They had unspoken rules and guidelines about courting relationships there. For instance, when a brother and sister started to court, the pastor should be notified right away, and never the last person to know. They would meet in the pastor's office, let him/her know about their relationship and receive pastoral covering. When engaged, they would meet with the pastor again to receive his/her blessing, and be introduced to the congregation as an engaged couple. It was beautiful to watch and I looked forward to experiencing my own engagement in that fashion. Unfortunately, it didn't work out that way.

Peter's Conversation with My Pastor

Peter and I still lived a great distance apart, which made it difficult for us to see each other often enough. So, I found him a basement apartment close to where I lived and he would come over to my place for dinner. One particular evening, a brother that I knew from my church called at ten o'clock. Peter was not thrilled about it. The next day, I was at work when I sensed that something was going on; however, I couldn't put my finger on it until I got home. Peter was over for dinner and I asked how his day was. This is when he told me about his conversation with my pastor. "What do you mean you had a conversation with my pastor?" I said. "My pastor doesn't even know who you are yet. What did you call him to say?"

"I told him that I am courting you and he needs to have more control over the brothers in his church." He continued, "They should not be calling sisters late at night" (SRW Signal #5).

"You did what?!" I said. I was livid. He took the one opportunity I had to share our relationship with my pastor away from me. This was especially hurtful since he knew how important it was for me to do so. To make a long story shorter, my pastor was not pleased, and wondered why I didn't tell him sooner about our relationship. I was so embarrassed and felt like I had no one to talk to, so I decided to leave the church (SRW Signal #5). Peter didn't like me going there anyway.

Peter shared his desire to marry me many times but not without telling me the type of woman he wanted me to be. For the next three years of our relationship, I allowed Peter to mould me into his ideal woman (SRW Signal #6). He had his own understanding of Scriptures and taught me his interpretation of them (SRW Signal #2). BIG MISTAKE! Remember that call to ministry I mentioned earlier? Well I made the mistake of sharing it with Peter. His response was "Women are never called to teach or preach. They are to be silent!" He also showed me Scripture to back this up. *"But I suffer not a woman to teach, nor to usurp authority over the man, but to be in silence"* (1 Timothy 2:12). Now I was even more confused (SRW Signal #8, #2).

When I visited Peter's church, it started to make sense. His entire family grew up with this understanding of Scripture. Women are not allowed to preach or teach inside the church period. This is what Peter saw and accepted. This wasn't the case for me. It was the exact opposite. I grew up seeing men and woman evangelists, preaching and teaching all the time. I tried to explain this to Peter but he made it clear; "I was under false teaching" (SRW Signal #4). At the time when Peter told me this, I was attending a church where there were female pastors and evangelists there. Soon, Peter's convictions became mine and I decided to leave this church too. But not before telling Bishop Dean, that he was wrong for ordaining women as elders/pastors (SRW Signal #6). I was headed for another collision and didn't even know it: *"Touch not mine anointed, and do my prophets no harm"* (Psalm 105:15).

In my mind, my goal was to be married by age twenty-seven. So, I tried my best to do and say everything right to impress Peter. But in his opinion, I was still too "combative." When I didn't go along with everything he said, he would often remind me of what Ephesians 5:24 says a wife is to submit herself to her husband in everything (SRW Signal #2). We had our disputes about this Scripture. Looking back now, I know this Scripture did not apply to us because we were not married. But being twenty-six and one year away from the goal, I didn't want to be disqualified from getting that ring, so I became his "Yes" woman. Soon my desire to please God was a desire of the past and pleasing Peter became my first priority (SRW Signal #6).

Still Church Hopping

Do you feel like you're on a roller coaster yet? Maybe now you will. I found yet another church and as far as I knew they only had men pastors and ministers...or so I thought. The day Peter decided to attend church with me, we heard the following: "Today we have a special speaker who will bring forth the message...her name is..." "Oh my God!" I said aloud. Peter looked at me, picked up his Bible and walked out of the church. I sat there thinking, "Is it really that bad for a woman to preach?" I waited until she finished her opening prayer and then quietly slipped out the door. When I got inside the car with Peter, he said, "You are not going to have me sitting under a woman preacher; and when I leave, you are supposed to leave with me. We are to be one!" He continued, "Why did you stay so long?" Then I replied, "Peter, I really don't know what the big deal is for a woman to preach the gospel. The Holy Spirit can speak through anyone, even a donkey!" To make a long story short, I never went back to that church again (SRW Signal #6).

Like Samson, I was beginning to lose my strength. But in the name of love I kept moving forward (SRW Signal #6). Peter moved back home, so our relationship again became a long distance one. Like most long distance relationships, we spent a lot of time talking on the phone and visiting each other on long weekends. By this time, we were together for seven years. There was nothing holy about our visits. He couldn't wait and I gave in (SRW Signal #5); we became fornicators. (In case you don't know what this means, it's a term used for people that have sex outside of marriage.)

To bring glory to our shame, Peter decided to pop the question in our hotel room. I was a shipwreck spiritually, emotionally, and physically, but went ahead anyway and accepted his proposal (SRW Signal #6). "How did I get here?" I thought. I didn't know who I was anymore. I lost myself completely in Peter and didn't know how to get myself back. When I told my family about my engagement they tried to be happy for me, but I saw right through them. They were just as unsure about Peter as I was beginning to feel.

Have you ever been at a place where you knew what you had to do but lacked the courage and strength to do it? Well, this is exactly where I was (SRW Signal #1). "What if I never met another man again?" "What if I make a mistake by letting him go?" These were just some of the thoughts that were going through my head. My fears and insecurities kept me bound to this relationship. I became an idol worshipper and didn't even know it. *"Do not worship any other god, for the LORD, whose name is Jealous, is a jealous God"* (Exodus 34:14 NIV). There were many times God tried to guide me away from this relationship, but I kept going back as if I didn't have any control over the matter. I was in a serious stronghold (SRW Signal #5).

SRW Words of Caution:

When we refuse to follow the leading of the Holy Spirit in our lives and want to have our own way, His voice begins to fade and soon we are left to discover the error of our ways.

Sin Will Take You Further Than You Bargained For

I was the spiritual "strong one" in my family; the one who always did the encouraging. Oh how quickly this changed. *"No man can enter into a strong man's house, and spoil his goods, except he will first bind the strong man; and then he will spoil his house"* (Mark 3:27). The verse couldn't have been any more real to me. My relationship with Peter sapped all my strength and it was starting to affect the members of my family too.

The more I continued to go in the wrong direction the worse my situation got. Prior to our engagement I lost my job, my unemployment insurance ran out, I ended up on social assistance for the first time and acne took over my entire face. I know that things like these happen every day, but looking back, I know they were a result of the disobedient lifestyle I was living. Then to bring glory to our shame like I mentioned before, Peter wanted us to get married as soon as possible (SRW Signal #1, #3, #4, #6).

My Situation Got Worse

My peace was gone and so was my joy. I was so confused and I remember thinking, "I am too young to be going through this." Then my situation got even worse! One evening my sister told me about a visiting prophetess that was in town and that maybe I should go. I hadn't been out all day so I decided to attend. While getting ready I felt as though I shouldn't go, but went anyway (SRW Signal #6). By this time, I was accustomed to not obeying the Holy Spirit but I needed a word from the Lord. I got a word all right! Well, not just yet. As I proceeded to leave, the visiting prophetess touched my face and said, "What a pretty girl!" I said thank you and left the church building.

A Word Came

Then it happened; I had the worst nightmare of my life. Right before dawn, I dreamt that I had my hands in the air reaching out for a word from God and then all of a sudden I was sitting right in front of that prophetess. She looked at me and said, "Enough is enough, you're going to die!" The dream ended and I woke up in a sweat, paralyzed by fear. From that same day, severe insomnia kicked in; and for the next seven months, I did not know what sleep was, as I did not have any. Some of you may find this hard to believe, but it really happened. My acne worsened and I couldn't keep my food down. My clothes began to pile up in garbage bags, I stopped going to church, combing my hair, was losing the desire to live, and I couldn't focus my mind very well. Reading anything was out of the question. Although I was in no shape to work, when I made an attempt to start looking, my computer completely shut down. I honestly felt like I was cursed and God had written me off for good. It was at this point that I really realized where my true joy came from. It wasn't from pleasing man or accumulating things, it was from my personal relationship with Christ and walking in obedience to His will.

My dear mother had no idea what was going on with me. Every day there was a new occurrence. On this one particular morning, I felt numb all over and my brother brought me to the hospital. We waited for hours before I was finally seen. They ran a number of tests and said that everything looked fine. When I got back home, my mother was distraught. All I could remember her saying in her Jamaican accent was, "But Jesus, I never see anyting like dis from de day mi bawn." (Translation: I haven't seen anything like this in my entire life.) Then she made the call I was dreading; a call to my father in Jamaica. After many attempts to get me to the phone, my dad suggested she take me to the Mount Sinai Hospital immediately for help. I didn't want to go, but went to make my mother feel better.

Mount Sinai Hospital

I sat in a room for some time at the hospital until a man wearing a white coat came in to talk to me. He was from the psychiatric ward. For some weird reason, he began speaking to me in a very soft and low voice. This spooked me out. I might have looked like I lost my marbles, but I still had some of my right mind left. Then he proceeded to ask me questions and suggested that I stay for the night. I replied, "I am not depressed, I don't plan on taking any medication, and I'm not staying the night. Where is my mom?" (To the world I looked depressed and maybe I was. Personally, I felt there was something more going on, but I wasn't sure.) He went to get my mother and they both came back trying to convince me to stay, at least for the night. I refused and started walking towards the door.

With each passing day it continued to get worse. Now the weirdest things began happening to me.

- ✓ I felt an evil presence that kept telling me I was going to hell.
- ✓ I was numb and couldn't feel any pain, so I was tempted to start cutting myself.
- ✓ I sat only on the floor. This is where I felt most comfortable for some reason.

✓I couldn't listen to anointed preachers without
  my ears hurting.

I experienced these things for months. I don't know how I
didn't end up losing the rest of my mind.

I Was a Prodigal Daughter

Trying to help, my mom asked me a question that I will
never forget. She said, "Tanika, what do you want? Do you
want me to get you a gym membership?" (I used to go to the
gym all the time). I didn't answer because I knew what I
needed, and she couldn't give it to me. I wanted my relationship with Jesus back. Deep down, I couldn't help to think if
this was exactly where God wanted me to be so I would see
where my will would take me. I was beginning to feel like the
prodigal son, who left his father's house to do his own thing
and returned when he realized how far he fell from grace.

While all these things were taking place with me, Peter
was unaware of the full extent of my situation. When I
spoke to him, his solution was always the same. "Why are
you fighting against God's will for us to be married, don't
you know everything is going to be fine when we do?" When
I got to my very lowest I remembered his words and
thought, what do I have to lose, I have nothing left to live
for (SRW Signal #6).

Dead End

I finally made the decision to go away and marry Peter
secretly (SRW Signal #6), so I did not even tell my mother.
However, God was still watching over me and had a better
plan for my life. Three days before leaving town to marry
Peter I got a call from a concerned sister from Bishop Dean's

31

church. I picked up the phone and she said, "Tanika?" I was quiet because I knew who was calling. She knew about my relationship with Peter and had instructed me during the course of my relationship to end it.

"Hi Wendy," I said.

She asked, "Where have you been? I heard you are no longer at Bishop Dean's church, what is going on with you? Why aren't you there anymore?"

I said to her, "I told the bishop he was wrong for having female elders/pastors and then I left."

"Is Peter still in the picture?" she asked.

"Yes," I said in a very weak voice. (Not sleeping for seven months was starting to take a toll on me.)

She continued, "You listen to me Tanika and you listen to me good! You have been on my mind for some weeks now and I just felt led to call you" (SRW Signal # 7). This call changed the direction of my life forever. She continued, "I was reading about Miriam and Aaron in the book of Numbers and didn't understand why until now." Miriam and Aaron questioned Moses' spiritual authority after looking at his unimpressive wife, who was an Ethiopian woman. God judged Miriam for initiating such an affront to his servant Moses, by giving her leprosy. However, Moses forgave Miriam and prayed to God for her healing. He prayed: "*Heal her now, O God, I beseech thee.*" God healed Miriam's leprosy and then told Moses to shut her out of the camp for seven days as a punishment (Numbers 12:13–14). "Tanika, I want you to do three things" (SRW Signal # 10).

1. End that relationship with Peter immediately.

2. Go to Bishop Dean and ask for forgiveness.

3. Cry out to God.

I knew it was God using my friend to reach out to me. So I obeyed and did everything she said to do (SRW Signal #9). Peter didn't handle it too well, but for the first time in a while I knew that I had to do what was right. The moment I returned home from asking Bishop Dean for forgiveness, I cried out to God with genuine repentance, and He heard my cry. You have to understand; in the seven months that I didn't sleep I also couldn't cry. I tried, but not a single tear would leave my eye. They were dry like a desert. However, that night as I cried out, tears began rolling down my face like a river, and I knew that the process of restoration had begun. I continued to call out to God and I heard the Holy Spirit say: "*If you are willing and obedient, you will eat the best from the land*" (Isaiah 1:19 NIV). "Yes Lord, I am willing...I am willing," I said with tears still running down my face. Everything I lost came back that night: my faith, the joy of my salvation, my strength, my hope, my prayer life, the confidence that I was saved, and my sleep pattern. "*If the Son therefore shall make you free, ye shall be free indeed*" (John 8:36).

The day I went back to Bishop Deans church I received a special word from the Lord. Coincidentally, it was Resurrection Sunday and like Lazarus, I felt that God brought me back to life from being spiritually dead. During the worship service, I heard a still small voice say, "Tanika, I am taking you from believing to knowing." God increased His wisdom and discernment in my life like never before.

Had I gone ahead and married Peter, I don't believe I would be alive today. Like David, I also say it was good for me to be afflicted so that I would learn His decrees (Psalm 119:71).

"The devil uses situations to destroy you, but God uses the same situations to develop you."—Pastor Orim Meikle

 **Are You Truly Single?**

If you want to have a successful courtship you must first look at what you bring to the road. Are you in the right condition to sit behind the courting wheel? Let's find out.

There is much more to being single than a person that is unattached.

The SRW definition of being truly single is: whole without holes.

What do I mean by whole without holes?

Have you ever placed loose change into your pocket, only to have them fall out because of a hole? Well, the same can be said about entering a courting relationship without first dealing with any unhealed wounds from your past. It can negatively affect your future relationship. So, to avoid this from happening you need to be whole without holes. Being "whole without holes" means you have the inner assurance that you have been made "whole" through the finished work on the cross! You are at a place in your life where you are ready to receive, maintain and keep the blessings/person that God brings into your life. You would have forgiven yourself for any wrongdoing on your part. Also, you would have been healed emotionally, mentally and spiritually, from the actions of all those who may have hurt or disappointed you in the past. Do you see yourself in this description? Whether you do or not, this STOP will confirm what you already know and have done, or assist you in getting there.

How do we become whole without holes?

The first thing I had to do on my journey to becoming whole was to let go of anything that held me to my past. Although I had broken up with Peter, I was still holding on to him in my heart. Then it happened; I remember the day as if it was yesterday. In my time of restoration God blessed me with a new job at the Canadian Bible Society. Being in this Christian environment was exactly what I needed. It was as though God was tangibly showing me that He was healing me through His Word.

The Release

I was at my desk working and the Holy Spirit began to minister to my heart saying, "it is time to let go." When the weight of those words grabbed a hold of my heart, tears began rolling down my face. In that moment, I knew what the Holy Spirit was telling me to do. So I walked over to my co-worker and asked if she could pray with me. After sharing a brief synopsis of why I was crying, I told her that I was ready to let go of my past and embrace the future with hope. Upon that confession she agreed with me in prayer and I received a release in my spirit like never before (SRW Signal #3). "*Stand fast therefore in the liberty wherewith Christ hath made us free, and be not entangled again with the yoke of bondage*" (Galatians 5:1).

What about you?

Have you really gotten over your ex (former relationship)? No matter how many times you may tell yourself and others that you are single, it isn't true if you haven't really let go of the person you were in a relationship with. "*Behold, thou desirest truth in the inward parts: and in the hidden part thou shalt make me to know wisdom*" (Psalm 51:6). In order to make room for a new and better relationship you have to be willing to let go of the old. You cannot be double minded in your single walk. "*A double minded man is unstable in all his ways*" (James 1:8).

Time to Really Let Go

Letting go of old relationships can be easier said than done. You have invested years of your life with someone who you thought would be "the one." However, now you have to move on without him/her. After receiving my release, I realized that there were still some things that I needed to do. They were:

1. Really End It.

Once you know that this man or woman is not who you are going to marry you need to really end it. This means no calling, texting, e-mailing or hanging out. What is the purpose in continuing to do that? The danger in staying connected, even as friends, is you could be drawn in again and the next thing you know you are back together for the fourth time; especially if the breakup was not mutual. If it didn't work the first, second, or third time chances are it is not a relationship you are meant to be in. However, if children are involved, a platonic friendship with their dad/mom is in the best interest of the child's development.

2. Get Rid Of Stuff.

You know the stuff they bought you, i.e., a teddy bear, necklace, ring, to name a few. Well things like these have a way of reminding us of "when." If being single is your goal then it would be best to get rid of these reminders that can be more of a distraction when you're trying to move forward with your life.

3. Break Soul-Ties.

"A soul-tie is an unhealthy connection with another person. You allow the person to control you in certain areas. You begin to lose your individuality and self-confidence. You let the person make decisions for you, or you base your decisions on what you think the person wants you to do. If the person is really good at manipulation, you will think that he or she is spiritually superior and will let him or her tell you what God is saying to you. The longer a relationship is unhealthy, the stronger the soul-tie will be."(Adapted from healingprayer.wordpress.com/preparation -of-family-tree/) (This could be a relationship where sex was involved or a non-sexual one where a stronghold was formed.) If you are planning to be married one day, it is especially important that you break free from soul-ties and strongholds to ensure that your marriage bed includes you, your spouse and God alone. "*If the Son therefore shall make you free, ye shall be free indeed*" (John 8:36). (To break a soul-tie, see the prayer at the end of this book.)

Other than an ex, is there anything else you need to let go of?

Is there a friend or family member that hurt you that you still need to forgive? Well, whatever it might be, for this journey you cannot carry it with you. Now is the time to let it go.

Single Journey Continues

Before we enter into a courting relationship, it helps to know who you are.

Who am I and what is my purpose in life?

Do you remember fourth grade and drawing stick images of your family members? Although very elementary, these exercises were in place to help us identify and understand the different roles we play in life (for example, you're a sister, brother, daughter, or son). When it comes to knowing who we are it is not a one time event; instead it is a process that spans over a lifetime because we are constantly growing and changing ourselves. Who we are today, may not be who we will be three years from now. For this reason, you want to have an idea of what your purpose is, preferably before entering a courting relationship with someone.

The kind of purpose that I am referring to is not your job, your daily responsibilities, or even your long-term goals. It is the real reason you are here on earth. Other than being a witness for Christ, what are you most passionate about? Could it be helping people? If so, in what areas: men, women, finances, healthcare, or childcare? What if your purpose is to be a pastor, evangelist, teacher, preacher, or missionary etc., have you taken the time to know for sure? *"Seek the LORD while he may be found; call on him while he is near"* (Isaiah 55:6 NIV). *"Keep on asking, and you will be given what you ask for. Keep on looking, and you will find. Keep on knocking, and the door will be opened"* (Matthew 7:7 NLT). Once you are aware of what this is, guard it, nurture it and develop it during your single season. When you marry already knowing what your calling and passion/purpose is, your marriage will be that more fulfilling as you support and encourage one another.

SRW Word of Caution:

If you are trying to know who you are, you will not find it in Sally or Bob. God is the only one that you can lose yourself in and find yourself. *"For whosoever will save his life shall lose it: and whosoever will lose his life for my sake shall find it"* (Matthew 16:25).

Love

Do I love and accept myself?

"'Love your neighbor as yourself.' There is no commandment greater than these" (Mark 12:31 NIV).

When it comes to loving yourself, pay close attention to the words you say and the thoughts you think about yourself. Many say or have thoughts like, "I'm not good enough," "Not pretty/handsome enough," "Not thin enough," "Not smart enough," and I can go on and on. When you say or think words or thoughts like these you are not thinking positively about yourself, nor are you showing self-love. As a single it is very important that you love and appreciate yourself before entering into a courting relationship. Otherwise, it can become a burden that you place on another when it is not their burden to carry. Learn to speak and think positive thoughts and words about yourself by reading the word of God and believing what it says about you.

"I praise you because I am fearfully and wonderfully made; your works are wonderful, I know that full well" (Psalm 139:14 NIV).

Do you know that God took the time to create you? Learn to love your wonderful and fearfully made self and don't compare yourself to others. When you learn to accept who you are you will be able to love and accept the person God has for you.

Do you always feel the need to be around others because you don't enjoy your own company? If so, do not turn a blind eye to this. It means you are not yet truly single. The day you make yourself smile or laugh while sitting home alone or on a park bench somewhere will be the day that you are becoming truly single; whole without holes in this area.

Early Childhood

Can a lack of love and acceptance from one's parent(s) at an early age affect how someone loves and accepts themselves later in life? Most definitely, while it would be wonderful if we all came from a home where we felt loved and accepted, this is not always the case. However, God promises that "*When my father and my mother forsake me, then the LORD will take me up*" (Psalm 27:10). In other words, God will make sure that you're taken care of, should your mother and father want nothing to do with you.

When my father moved to Jamaica he wasn't around when I needed him most. But God, in His loving care did not leave me fatherless. When I started to attend Bishop Dean's church something special took place. This was the first time I knew what a spiritual father was. I respected Bishop Dean and often felt like one of his daughters. If you remember my story, this was the second church I went to, which goes to show that, even in our mess, God can still work everything out for our good. "*And we know that all things work together for good to them that love God, to them who are the called according to his purpose*" (Romans 8:28).

Whether you have been forsaken by a parent or lost a parent by death, when you need it most God will bring others into your life to fill that void. This is His way of saying I will never leave or forsake you. *"Be strong and courageous. Do not be afraid or terrified because of them, for the LORD your God goes with you; he will never leave you nor forsake you"* (Deuteronomy 31:6 NIV). If you grew up feeling unloved by a parent, I encourage you to forgive them today. Forgive them for leaving you at a young age, forgive them for not being there when you needed them most, and make the choice to walk in love. This is all part of becoming truly single and whole without holes.

Am I Happy or Do I Have Joy?

Yes it's true, happiness does depend on one's circumstances. But this is not the case for joy. You not only want to be happy with who you are before courtship, you want to have your own sense of joy too. In my humble opinion, joy apart from a personal relationship with God is meaningless. Money can't buy it, a person can't give it and the world definitely cannot take it away. It is an emotion you feel when you're walking in obedience to God. One that I hope you are experiencing right now. The joy of the Lord is your strength (Nehemiah 8:10).

Are You Single Again?

Although I haven't experienced divorce on a personal level, this question was included if you have.

If you were married for an extended period of time and are single again consider this "SRW Single Again Self Checklist" to re-evaluate your thoughts and feelings and where you could be right now.

✓Why did my marriage come to an end?

✓Could this marriage be reconciled?

✓If I initiated the divorce why did my" I do" turn into "I don't"?

✓Did I attend marriage counseling to try and save the marriage?

✓Have I healed emotionally from the divorce?

✓Have I taken the time to reflect and take responsibility for where I might have gone wrong in the marriage?

✓Am I truly single: whole without holes?

✓If I entertain a new relationship right now and my divorce is not yet finalized will it affect my relationship with God, my church and those that look up to me?

They say time heals all wounds, but if you have been grieving the loss of a spouse for an extended amount of time I would suggest finding a Christian counselor to help you with your grief. God wants you whole and ready to receive all that he still has in store for you. "*He is despised and rejected of men; a man of sorrows, and acquainted with grief: and we hid as it were our faces from him; he was despised, and we esteemed him not*" (Isaiah 53:3).

For additional resources on how to successfully move on after divorce and the Biblical grounds for divorce and remarriage visit my website:

www.singlereadyandwaiting.com.

As you can see, the process to becoming truly single takes time, reflection, and honesty with yourself, and if you're willing to do the work, you will be ready to handle the next STOP towards courtship. "*Being confident of this, that he who began a good work in you will carry it on to comple-tion until the day of Christ Jesus"* (Philippians 1: 6 NIV).

Are You Dating or Courting?

In order to drive on this road you need to know which lane you're going to drive in.

This was the question I asked myself a year after my relationship with Peter ended. I had begun to date again, but wasn't interested in going out on multiple dates with a mindset of "seeing where things would go." So, I made the decision to focus completely on my relationship with God, stop dating, pursue purpose, and enjoy life as best as I could. I also took some time to discover the type of man I wanted to marry.

I Kissed Dating Goodbye

The day I kissed dating goodbye (a challenging book written by Joshua Harris), I knew that I was no longer part of the majority. Choosing not to date in today's society is just unheard of. If you're not dating, something must be wrong with you. You're either considered gay, strange, or sheltered. Personally, it was the best decision I ever made.

"Don't you have to date to find a mate?" You might ask. Absolutely not, but this is exactly what our secular dating system suggests. One must go through a series of relationships in order to find love. The problem with this ideology is that accidents and collisions can occur and the results can seem worse than death; you may end up living with a broken heart.

What are some of the reasons why people date?

✓They are looking for a husband/wife

✓They are lonely

✓Peer pressure—family and friends

✓The society and culture we live in makes people think they are supposed to

✓Something to do to pass time

✓Just for fun

✓Sex without commitment

Do you date? What is your reason for dating?

If your reason for dating is to find a mate this is a good thing. But, dating alone is not going to prepare you for marriage. Instead of dating, STOP and see where you're at emotionally, intellectually, and spiritually. Then, WAIT and prepare by getting the right mindset for courtship. Afterwards, GO! Court the right man or woman after praying and getting God's green light. This way you will avoid accidents and collisions along the way and arrive safely to your final destination: "marriage."

In and out of Christendom the words *dating* and *courting* have been used interchangeably so much that people have lost the true meaning of what it means to be in a "courting relationship." Unlike dating, a courting relationship has the following component: "**intent to marry**." Now you're probably thinking if dating is a no-no, how does one get to know someone before entering a courting relationship? The SRW answer to this question is: **pursue a friendship first.**

Friendship Stage

Building a friendship first before entering a courtship is like pouring cement to build the foundation of a house. Without it the house could not stand strong and firm. When you allow your friendship to develop with what I call the "SRW Hands-off Approach," which is no touching (in a sexual way) or kissing, a pure friendship can be made. Doing this will form a strong, firm and respectable foundation for a possible courtship, then marriage relationship.

Chris Sanders, a former player for the NFL's Tennessee Titans, was quoted saying, "Too often, we focus on kissing someone's mouth instead of focusing on what comes out of his or her mouth."

What do you think is the best way to get to know someone?

If you said over the phone, in public places or in group settings, I would agree with you. When driving, you should be conscious of the road conditions and positions of other vehicles while changing lanes and making turns, so that you drive accordingly and therefore stand a better chance of not getting into accidents. The same can be said about the stage of "friendship." You have to be very conscious of where you go alone together and for how long, making sure to take all the necessary precautions to avoid what could also be termed as "accidents." So for example, while you are in this stage you have to be very careful of even a late night visit to each other's home, innocent as it may seem. Because if you are not careful, it could turn out to be more than either of you thought about, or planned.

What are the benefits of keeping a friendship pure?

✓No regrets

✓Your friendship won't be "complicated" with physical intimacy

✓Your mind can be focused on what matters most: getting to know them (their values, beliefs and whether you are equally yoked).

Having gone through that courtship collision, I was more determined than ever to not repeat the same mistakes twice. I would ask the right questions and take my time in getting to know him as a friend.

Four years later, this was exactly what I did when I met Robert. When he passed my interview questions with flying colours our friendship started. We had a lot in common and enjoyed being in each other's presence. Then at the right time a courting relationship developed out of our friendship. All the time we spent over the phone, out on lunches and walks by the boardwalk (sounds like a personal classified doesn't it?) during our season of courtship are the memories we share and draw strength from today as a married couple. When you decide to build memories with someone that you intend to marry, it really makes your coming together that more special.

What makes courting more scriptural than dating?

While dating and courting are not found in the Bible, courtship is more scriptural than dating because courting is with the intent to marry like I previously mentioned. For example, in the story of Adam and Eve, there was no mention of romantic feelings like our secular dating system suggests, only of needs. Their union was the perfect example of God's intent for marriage; women and men are to live as partners and their togetherness has a purpose.

Another couple that reveals God's intent for marriage is Isaac and Rebekah.

When Abraham felt it was time for Isaac, his son, to marry he sent for his most trusted servant and told him to find a suitable mate, but not before giving his servant specific instructions to make the search a success. Abraham's requirements were: A young woman from his homeland, Aram Nahariam, beautiful, pure, hospitable, accommodating, polite and perceptive. (I wonder if this is where the idea of writing a list came from.) As the story unfolds, the servant actually encounters a young woman named Rebekah who meets all of Abraham's requests and, as divine providence would have it, Rebekah not only met the criteria, she also happened to be from the right tribe (in modern terms of the same faith). They got married and came to love each other very much (Genesis 24 1–67).

In addition, we not only see the intent to marry in that particular story, but we also find another facet to courting relationships: the release—blessing or permission from a spiritual father to court someone. Unfortunately, with the fall of many pastors, also known as a shepherd in the Bible, within the last decade people have been looking less and less to spiritual leaders for guidance when making personal decisions like courtship. However, despite what is happening, there are pastors who are in right standing with God and take their roles very seriously, wanting nothing more than God's best for their sheep.

From experience, I recommend talking to an elder, pastor/spiritual father, or minister about a person you are interested in courting; no matter how young or old you are.

A pastor's role is to watch over themselves and all of their flock to which the Holy Spirit has made them overseers (Acts 20:28). Therefore, a good spiritual leader will not only uphold you and your relationship in prayer they will offer helpful advice and guidance or direct you to someone who can, should their schedule not permit it. If you don't have an elder, pastor/spiritual father then another alternative would be someone you look up to spiritually that you trust.

While spiritual counsel is recommended, God is always the first one to counsel with for direction. He's the only one that really knows the end from the beginning (Isaiah 46:10).

When should you seek spiritual guidance?

The moment you begin to get to know someone—God says "*in all your ways acknowledge him, and he will make your paths straight*" (Proverbs 3:6 NIV)—take it to God in prayer. It was only two weeks, when I decided to let my pastor know about Robert. I knew there was something special about him and how we met. Now, I'm not suggesting that you let your pastor know about everyone you meet, but if you sense that there is something special about him/her, and you have this kind of relationship with your pastor, it wouldn't hurt to fill them in.

Now I ask you, what are your intentions? If God were to tell you that next year this time He would bless you with a mate, would you wait? What would you do in the meantime? Well, whether your wait is one year or five years, the truth remains the same: to receive God's best, you have to work on being truly single—whole without holes—and become the best you.

Are You Truly Ready?

Once you have obeyed the "Red Signal Light" by coming to a complete STOP and making sure that you are truly "single," you are more than welcome to get into your car and put your hands on the wheel. Soon, you will be able to travel on the highway but until then, proceed with caution.

Slow It Down

Say you're supposed to start work at 8:30 a.m. but you forgot to set your alarm so you wake up at 8:00 a.m. You get a quick shower, throw on some clothes, comb your hair, put on your shoes and jump into the car. As you drive down the road you realize you forgot your lunch on the kitchen counter. You speed down the street hoping and praying for green lights, only to be confronted with an "amber signal light" that is about to turn red. You foresee that you won't make it in on time so you decide to accelerate on the gas but end up running the red light. You continue to speed ahead when you don't see a police officer in sight. Since you are the chairman for the morning's meeting, you call into work to let your supervisor know you're running late. Her response puts you at ease: "Take your time, its better that you get here safely than to rush and end up in a collision along the way. Don't worry; I'll chair the meeting until you get here. See you soon." Now your drive takes on a more relaxed approach.

Does this story sound familiar to you? Well, like the response of the supervisor in the above illustration, courtship leading to marriage is the goal and you want to get there safely without casualties. Having learned the consequences of not obeying the true guide behind the "SRW Signals"—the Holy Spirit, I realized just how really important the signals are at every stage, especially this one.

In order to have a successful courting relationship you have to be truly Ready for it, be with the right person, at the right time…three factors that can be easily overlooked if you are not careful. In order to avoid your own collision, get familiar with these three equations:

NOT READY + WRONG PERSON =
COLLISION…waiting to happen.

READY + WRONG PERSON =
COLLISION…waiting to happen.

READY + RIGHT PERSON + WRONG TIME
= COLLISION…waiting to happen.

Based on the above, does anyone come to mind? Did you experience a collision because you or the person you were with was not truly Ready for it? If so, getting them a copy of this book would not be a bad idea.

What does it mean to be truly ready for a courting relationship?

Before answering this question, consider this one: when someone says they are a Christian do you believe them? Or do you wait for tangible signs that confirm their belief before believing they are saved? Well the same can be said of those that say they are ready. Saying that you're ready is one thing, and being ready is another. For this reason, it is important to have an idea of what being ready looks like.

Are You Truly R.E.A.D.Y.?

R—Red, the colour that can be found on one's bank account signifying a negative cash flow, loss, lack, which all mean he/she is facing financial difficulty.

While I am not a financial expert on the subject I don't have to be one to know that as powerful as love is, it cannot pay the bills. Never go into a courting relationship if you or the person you are considering is consistently experiencing a red bank account balance. This may not be the best time for you or them to consider a courting relationship.

Ladies, if you choose to stay with someone who is not yet financially stable, be prepared to handle what goes along with that. This could mean you won't have the wedding you've always dreamed about, and you might be the one paying for things until he gets a stable paying job. Instead of complaining about his financial status find ways to help; this is far more encouraging.

What do studies show on this topic?

Nearly all Americans in committed relationships (91 percent) agree that it is important to discuss their partner's financial history before marriage, yet more than one quarter (26 percent) admit they tend to avoid talking about finances.

Source: 2011 Lawyers.com

31% of those who combined finances admitted to lying to their spouses about money. Another third of those surveyed said they'd been deceived by their spouses.

Source: Online poll commissioned by ForbesWoman and the National Endowment for Financial Education (NEFE) and conducted by Harris Interactive. Source: Credit.com (http://s.tt/15Fn0).

86 percent of those who either got married in the past five years—or plan to get married in the next 12 months—say they plan on talking about money and their financial situations prior to the wedding.

Source: Online survey commissioned by the National Endowment for Financial Education (NEFE) and conducted by Harris Interactive in May 2011. Source: Credit.com (http://s.tt/15Fn0).

An American Express survey found that only 43 percent of the general population talked money before marriage, but the number rises to 57 percent for affluent couples and jumps to 81 percent for young professionals. And twelve percent of the general population says they've never talked about money with their spouse. How they manage that is definitely unclear.

Source: American Express Spending & Saving Tracker, June 2010. Source: Source: Credit.com (http://s.tt/15Fn0).

E—Every day pray and read God's Word for direction in your life. "*In all your ways acknowledge him, and he will make your paths straight*" (Proverbs 3:6 NIV). Whomever you hang out with the most will become the loudest voice you hear. There is your voice, someone else's voice, the devil's voice, and God's voice. When you choose to spend time with God and his Word you will not have to wonder who is speaking to you, you can know who's speaking! And, when you hear His voice you should not harden your heart towards it. *"For he is our God and we are the people of his pasture, the flock under his care. Today, if you hear his voice, do not harden your hearts"* (Psalm 95:7–8 NIV). *"My sheep hear my voice, and I know them, and they follow me"* (John 10:27).

Do you really want to know if he or she is the one? Remain in the secret place of prayer and don't assume what the Holy Spirit could be saying, like I made the mistake of doing. Take the time to be certain of the direction He could be leading you in. Had I not remained in that secret place the second time around I probably would not have been married today.

Practice Walking in Submission To God First

Walking in submission to God is easier said than done, but when we do the benefits are great. Being married for almost three years, I see why Robert and I work. We were both submitted to Christ before we began courting. Our desire was to please God then and that desire hasn't changed today. Ladies, only a man that is truly submitted to God will be able to love you the way you ought to be loved (like Christ loves the church), and men, only a woman that is truly submitted to God will be able to respect and reverence you the way God desires her to.

SRW Words of Caution:

Are you guilty of wanting a "God fearing man/woman" without being one yourself? Remember, whatever standards you hold to another person you should also possess.

There is no denying that a personal relationship with God is very important. Time spent with Him and His Word is never wasted time. It will allow you to discern the real "one" from any counterfeits that may come your way. Remain in His presence.

What do studies show on this topic?

In an interview with Assist News Service Rhodes quotes a recent poll, which indicates that 35% of born-again Christians do not read the Bible at all. In addition, Rhodes indicates that among those who say they read the Bible, the vast majority only read it during the one hour they attend church each Sunday morning. Rhodes says such statistics make it more than obvious why many Christians are easy prey for spiritual deception. The level of biblical illiteracy among Christians may be one reason why many believers hesitate to stand for godly values on the public scene.

Source: Assist News Service / Agape Press, 25/26 December.

A—Ask questions. How comfortable are you in asking for advice? Are you open to hearing positive criticism? To prepare for the stage of courtship you should consider and value the opinions of other mature Christians (a married couple in your church or family that you admire and respect), especially if you've made poor selections in the past. Their wisdom could help you to make a better choice in the future. What about another couple or single brother or sister you know? Do they have habits or character traits that you admire and would like to emulate or develop in yourself? Talk to them, maybe they can share a tip or two. What about cooking? Do you know how to cook? Why not ask someone that knows how? I'm sure they would be flattered by your request and wouldn't mind teaching you. Or maybe signing up for a cooking class in your area is not a bad idea. Are you a man and would like to know the right way to go about pursuing a woman? Then why not ask another married man or woman you respect for their advice and suggestions? You would be surprised to know what the ladies like.

Last but not least, what about asking your close friends and family what they really think about you? It will require a lot of confidence on your part but remember their advice is free and you can learn from it. Who knows, you might end up learning that you've been doing something that detracts instead of attracts people to you. Questions were made to be asked so never feel too proud or shy to ask them. "*As iron sharpens iron, so one man sharpens another*" (Proverbs 27:17 NIV).

D—Develop good character. Good character is not something you are born with; it is developed over time. It is the behaviour that you consistently do that becomes a habit in your life. Good character can bring opportunities your way and bad character can put you behind prison walls...literally. But the good news is this, we can all decide on the type of character we want to have and focus on developing that. Sure, you may have been dealt a bad hand in life, which causes you to act and behave the way you do, but this is still no excuse for not changing.

As Christians, it is God's desire to transform us into the image of His Son, Jesus Christ. I cannot think of a better place to start than Galatians 5:22–23. In this chapter we find the nine fruits of the spirit. They are "*love, joy, peace, patience, kindness, goodness, faithfulness, gentleness, and self-control*" (NLT). In order for a courtship or marriage to thrive, these fruits must be first and foremost operating in our lives. These fruits are developed as you face different situations involving people on the job, at home, in your family or at church, and you will have the opportunity to respond in one of these nine ways. This is why rushing into a courting relationship is not the way to go. When you take the time to get to know someone, opportunities will arise letting you know how he/she will react to different situations, which will in turn reveal his/her true character. Are you willing to be transformed by the Word of God as quoted in the above scripture? If you are, then your future spouse will thank you for doing so.

Y—Yes to boundaries. As a single, you have to prepare for the obvious; you will be approached by men/women that are not of your faith. Are you prepared to handle this? What will you say when/if you are approached? Will you consider entering a courting relationship with them? As a Christian, God has boundaries in place for your own good and when we decide not to abide by them we can end up losing more than we bargained for.

Samson in the book of Judges is a perfect example of this.

So she cried whenever she was with him and kept it up for the rest of the celebration. At last, on the seventh day, he told her the answer because of her persistent nagging. Then she gave the answer to the young men... Then Delilah pouted, "How can you say you love me when you don't confide in me? You've made fun of me three times now, and you still haven't told me what makes you so strong!" So day after day she nagged him until he couldn't stand it any longer" (Judges 14:17, 16:15-16 NLT).

Here we see Samson's dilemma. He fell in love with two Philistine women, whom God had forbidden the Israelites to court. Samson did not follow this forbidden command. He married the first woman, only to be manipulated and betrayed by her shortly after they wed. Then after nagging him so much for the secret answer to a riddle, he eventually told her. As a result, Samson ended up acting impulsively and stepped outside of God's will. Right when you think Samson learned his lesson, he finds himself in the same predicament with another Philistine woman named Delilah. She kept asking him to tell her what made him so strong and he refused to tell her. But, like the first woman, the nagging became unbearable, he gave in, revealed his secret, and lost his strength.

Do you want to lose your strength? Do you want to lose the anointing on your life? When you open yourself up to men and women that are not God's will for your life this is exactly what could happen. Saul lost his anointing and never did get it back. Even though David referred to him as "*the LORD's anointed*" (1 Sam 24:6, 26:9), we see that the anointing of the Lord left him, and rested upon David.

Ladies and gentlemen, while you prepare for the one you want to marry, be prepared to turn the wrong person away as well. You may wonder, "How will I know when it is the wrong person?" Well, the Holy Spirit will reveal this to you. However, there are also some obvious signs which I will call "SRW...No Trespassing Signs." When you obey them, you will be able to determine which ones are right/not right for you.

Here are some examples:

1. If you are a Christian then it is quite clear according to 2 Corinthians 6:14, that there are boundaries regarding who you marry. So courting a non-Christian would be outside of these boundaries.

2. Let's say he/she is a Christian but belongs to a different faith/denomination. Courting someone like this is clearly outside of your lane. To proceed with the hopes of them converting to your faith later on would mean you are missionary dating. There is no guarantee they will convert. It can also be considered as being unequally yoked (2 Corinthians 6:14). This is one missions trip I hope you don't take!

3. Then there are men and women who are within your faith/denomination but the Holy Spirit still waves the "No Trespassing sign." God obviously sees something that you don't, which makes them off-limits for you.

Couples That Ignored The No Trespassing Sign

These types of couples exist, they got married and are still married today, but they can tell you it has not been a smooth ride. Many of these attend church alone and or attend a different service on another day without their spouse. So, although they managed to make the marriage work, it was not the ideal situation. Remember, God wants His very best for you! So the more you obey these NO TRESPASSING signs the better off you will be.

Are We Ever Truly Ready?

This was the question I was asked during an interview when promoting this book and my answer was yes and no. Let me explain. Have you ever felt like you were not ready for a certain position at work, but your boss felt otherwise and you got the new position? Or what about feeling like you are ready, only to be told that you are not ready yet? Well, whether you have experienced the former or the latter, what is most important is that the potential of being ready, is present in both situations. Therefore, do not beat yourself up for not having all your T's crossed or your I's dotted. We are all a work in progress in need of God's grace. Over the next STOPS, the journey towards being ready continues. Apply what you have read so far and hold on to your seat. We are about to bump into some unpleasant potholes.

Beware of Potholes

What comes to mind when you think of a pothole? If you said a nuisance I couldn't agree with you more. Potholes can slow you down from getting to your destination, puncture your tire if you're trying to go too fast over them, and stop you in your tracks if unaware of them. In this book, potholes are disguised as wrong mindsets. They can slow you down and cause you to get stuck in or outside of a courting relationship. So how can you avoid having a pothole mentality? By knowing where they are.

Pothole # 1—Dating is a relationship

Those who believe that dating is a relationship can find themselves in a pothole. Reason being, dating is not a relationship but a method used to get to know someone. When you understand that dating is not a relationship you will do two things:

1. Guard your own heart (Proverbs 4:23).

2. Not awaken love before the right time (Song of Solomon 8:4).

If you choose to date (go out with different people) the best advice I can give you is this: don't allow your heart to go where your friendship isn't. This is where so many daters get hurt. They confuse the dating/friendship stage with that of a courting relationship, and then end up getting hurt when he/she decides they want to take an early EXIT. Trusting that he/she is not a player, but someone who is serious about meeting a soul mate, I would consider this to be the best time for him/her to know whether or not there is an interest in going any further, rather than saying so in a courting relationship where much time and energy have been invested. With a guarded heart and not awakening love before the time you will be able to handle a situation like this, understanding that he/she is looking for what you're looking for, "the one." If this friendship does not develop into a courting relationship, then you are both one step closer to meeting the right one.

Pothole #2—Failing to include God's counsel while getting to know someone

Have you ever made a decision without praying about it first, only to find out later it was not the right decision to make? Well this can be avoided if you acknowledge God in all of your ways, so He can direct your path (Proverbs 3:6). Building a close friendship with a "Courting potential" is no different. In fact, the best time to acknowledge God is at the very beginning of getting to know someone. Remember, while you are just getting to know him/her God already knows who he/she is.

When you ask God to order your steps, He will do just that. I will never forget the time when a friend of mine played matchmaker by introducing me to one of his friends. He was a Christian, studying to be a doctor, ambitious, and had a nice smile with pearly white teeth. (Nice teeth were on my list.) When I got home from our first double date I prayed to God about him. By the second date God told me he wasn't the one. I was not a happy camper. My conversation with God went like this:

"God did you hear or did you not hear that he is educated and studying to become a doctor?" "HELLOOOO!"

"Do you see that he is my type?" "HELLOOOO!"

"Do you see the way he opened the door for me and said all the right things?" "HELLOOO!"

God: "He's not the one."

A year later, I found out that he went back with his ex–girlfriend and got married. Who knows, I could have been that rebound girl had I not obeyed God's voice. Do you see how important it is to include God from the very beginning? He promises to be our guide when we continue to seek His direction. Our job is to LISTEN and OBEY what the Holy Spirit is saying.

Here is a simple prayer you can pray to include God from the beginning:

Lord, I thank You for allowing me and _____ to meet. As I get to know _____ I ask that You reveal the real purpose for our meeting and lead us by Your Spirit. In the meantime, I will guard my heart and not awaken love before the right time with Your help. Now, let Your perfect will be done in this friendship. Amen.

After praying a prayer like this, watch for the "SRW Signals" that will come and most importantly follow them. It is God's way of guiding you away from this person or towards courtship.

Pothole #3—Immaturity

Let's face it; some people are single because they are still immature. To be in a courting relationship it takes a level of maturity. One should ask themselves am I mature enough to be in a courting relationship?

If so, these five signs should follow them.

He/she:

✓Knows what they want in a partner as well as in life.

✓Takes life seriously.

✓Does not allow their emotions or feelings to determine their course of action.

✓Able to communicate their feelings effectively.

✓Can handle conflicts or disagreements effectively.

Another description of maturity can be found in 1 Corinthians 13:11. "*When I was a child, I spake as a child, I understood as a child, I thought as a child: but when I became a man [or woman], I put away childish things.*"

What if you or the person you're considering does not have all five signs, would it be a good idea to still enter a courting relationship?

If this question comes to mind the answer is yes and no. If someone is willing to learn and grow in the area(s) they need to mature in, then yes. But if he/she is not willing to acknowledge their immaturity in the areas they need to grow and develop then the answer is no. "*Brethren, be not children in understanding: howbeit in malice be ye children, but in understanding be men*" (1 Corinthians 14:20).

If you are in the pothole of immaturity all is not lost. While single, work on the areas that need to be worked on and prayerfully submit them to God. He will perfect those things that concern you.

Pothole #4—Putting the burden on someone else to love you. Love yourself first.

"'*Love the Lord your God with all your heart and with all your soul and with all your strength and with all your mind'; and, 'Love your neighbor as yourself*'" (Luke 10:27). So many find themselves in this pothole when they realize a person cannot give them what they need to give themselves: self-love. Prior to meeting Peter I struggled privately with self-confidence, self-esteem and self-worth. All of which could affect how someone loves themselves and the decisions they need to make in life. When my relationship with Peter ended the way it did, through God's divine intervention, I knew that I wasn't supposed to leave this world without experiencing what God ordained me to have—wholeness of life.

Coincidentally, my last name was "Holness" pronounced wholeness. For further understanding I looked up the definition of this word and found out that wholeness means "integrity: an undivided or unbroken completeness or totality with nothing wanting (http://www.thefreedictionary.com/wholeness). This spoke volumes to me and encouraged me even the more to become it. I stopped comparing myself to others that were prettier, more accomplished, had more money, and even those that had gotten married before me. Instead, I began telling myself that I was enough and my self-esteem, self-worth, and self-confidence increased because of it. I also stopped believing the lies of the enemy and allowed God's word to define who I was instead. Maybe this is where you are today, believing the lies that say you're not pretty enough, outgoing enough, thin enough, or fat enough? Well, today this could all change. If you find yourself in this pothole you too can become whole. Start by reading God's Word and believing what He says about you. *"And Peter said unto him, Aeneas, Jesus Christ maketh thee whole: arise, and make thy bed. And he arose immediately"* (Acts 9:34). Then accept and celebrate your uniqueness. You will walk much lighter and experience a sense of freedom you probably haven't felt in a long time.

Pothole #5—My happiness comes from being in a relationship.

Have you ever had a girlfriend that was miserable and moody most of the time but once they got "a man" they became happy and nice all of a sudden? POTHOLE! And then when there was friction in their relationship she made another switch. From Miss Nice to "Les Misérables," French for "the miserable." Is this person you or someone you know? Well no matter the case, this Jekyll and Hyde personality has got to go. If someone has this much power over another person's feelings, he/she should ask themselves, am I truly ready for a relationship? As a married woman I can tell you, there will be days when your spouse may do something that will make you feel unhappy, but this should only last for a moment. This mood should not control the rest of your day or affect the way you respond to others; you musn't allow it.

I will go even further by saying don't believe the lie that says you don't have any control over your emotions. God has given us all the ability to make choices. The best way to get out of this pothole is to first find out why you are unhappy outside of this relationship. Is it insecurity? If so, you will want to pay close attention to the next pothole. *"A false balance is not good"* (Proverbs 20:23).

Pothole # 6—Insecurity

Many, many people enter courting relationships and marriages feeling very insecure. The problem with this is they will become dependent on the other person to make them feel happy about themselves. (One of the root causes of a Jekyll and Hyde personality described in the previous pothole.)

How would you recognize an insecure person in a relationship?

1. The insecure person would always be looking to the other person in the relationship to provide him/her with a sense of completeness and happiness. He/she would also only feel happy when in a relationship.

2. There would be a lack of trust on this person's part as well, letting him/her always feeling the need to check up on the other person, even if there is no justification for it.

3. The insecure person is usually a "high maintenance" or (high needs) person, who constantly wants attention and love from the other person.

4. He/she is normally jealous, domineering, controlling, possessive, selfish and overprotective.

If you are this insecure person or maybe you are with an insecure person, either of you must make the decision to get free from this mindset today. Otherwise, it could negatively affect many aspects of your relationship, including even your offspring. Parents have a strong influence on their children, making this decision to deal with your insecurities another good reason to become whole in this area.

Having a secure self will attract other secure people to you. So the faster you repair this pothole the better.

The first steps to doing this would be to do the following:

1. Acknowledge that this is you.

2. Confess and pray for healing with a secure and trusted friend.

3. Or find a good Christian counselor to help you in overcoming your insecurities. This should enable you to acquire techniques in building your own self esteem, confidence and trustworthiness; so that you may have a normal and healthy relationship.

Ladies and gentlemen, please do all that you can to literally save yourselves from entering or staying in the wrong courting relationship. And, if you are in a courting relationship, do everything in your power right now to make it a better one!

Get secure!

Pothole #7—On-Again, Off-Again Relationship

Having been in this kind of relationship for eight years, trust me it is a roller coaster ride you don't want to be on. Looking back on my collision story, I take full responsibility for where I went wrong in the relationship. The on-again and off-again relationship was my doing. (Confession is good for the soul.) Although Peter was ready to marry me, I lacked the peace I needed to go forward with marrying him. But instead of breaking things off permanently I hung in there hoping that the peace would come; it never did.

Why do people stay in on-again, off-again relationships? Here are a number of reasons:

1. Love, causing one to neglect the red lights that are flashing.
2. Not sure if he/she is the right person they want to marry.
3. Not sure if they are truly ready to get married.
4. Fear of being alone.
5. They are in a stronghold due to a sexual or non-sexual soul-tie.

The reality of a consistently off and on again relationship is this: they don't often work out. When a relationship is not meant to be, waiting around to see if the peace or love is going to come is not going to happen. The best way to get out of this pothole is to accept what is really going on, and ask yourself these two questions: Is this relationship worth fighting for? And why are you putting up with this emotional roller coaster? If you're unsure, I would highly suggest finding a Christian counselor to help you figure this out.

Pothole #8 Do I have a phobia in regards to commitment?

This is definitely a question you need to ask yourself, especially if the words "until death do us part," cause you to feel like the walls are about to cave in. If you have a fear of commitment, you run the risk of sabotaging your relationship, even before you get the chance to have it developed into something meaningful. It can also be said that a

71

fear of commitment is a state of double-mindedness. If you are double minded in your single walk it means that you are not "Ready." Let's say that your true desire is to have a mate, and you meet someone with great potential, you may end up pushing this person away because of this mindset or cold feet. It makes absolutely no sense to want a mate, and not want a mate at the same time. So, to work your way out of this pothole you must ask yourself the question: Do I really want a meaningful relationship or am I only in love with the idea of being in one? If you feel that you are called to a life of singleness then commit to doing that. Never feel that you have to be in a relationship because the media, family or friends say so. Be like the apostle Paul and be content in your singleness. However, if you do not want a life of singleness, then before you proceed any further (to the next Stop), you need to get out of this "pothole" by dealing with your "phobia of commitment." Otherwise, you could miss out on having a great courting relationship that could lead to marriage. If you are having difficulty doing this on your own, seek out a Christian counselor and get the help you need to overcome this phobia, so that you will be ready to commit to a relationship, when the opportunity presents itself!

Pothole #9—Not married within 3 years or less

Three years or less is the ideal amount of time that a man or woman (23 yrs old and over) should be together before walking down the aisle. This includes building a solid friendship and a season of courtship. Anything longer can indicate the following: they are not the right person for you or they were not truly ready when you met them. When you meet the right one it does not take you long to find this out. You will experience what so many married couples told me before I tied the knot: "You will just know." They were right. I had a sense of knowing that Robert was the one, along with these **5 telltale signs** that I believe could assist you too.

1. Is he/she different from any other person you have been in a relationship with?

When I say different I mean this in a positive way. Unlike the individual(s) you might have encountered in the past.

✓They are not the controlling or manipulating type?

✓They are ready to make a commitment?

✓They are someone you can be yourself with?

✓They desire to please God?

✓They are patient, understanding and make time in their busy schedule to get to know you?

✓They are emotionally, spiritually and financially stable?

✓Being in their presence encourages you to walk closer to God?

Then, he or she will be worth your time and effort. Remain prayerful and continue to get to know him/her.

2. When what he/she does impresses you more than what he/she says.

Sure he or she can hold an intellectual conversation. But can they remember your best friend's name? Or remember what your favourite food is and surprise you with it? Or help you study for your upcoming exam? And what about how they react when you share your thoughts and point of views? Do they roll their eyes and quickly change the subject? If they go out of their way for you, show interest and attention to what you have to say, this is another good sign. Remain prayerful and continue to get to know him/her.

3. They make you feel great about yourself.

I truly believe that the right person could improve your self-respect, self-esteem and self-confidence and the wrong person can do the opposite. If he/she makes you feel special in private and in public, is not afraid to let you know how they feel, compliments you, focuses on your positives rather than your negatives this is also a very good sign. No one wants to be around someone that constantly puts them down and does not appreciate their value or doesn't care to know anything about them. Remain prayerful and continue to get to know him/her.

4. You feel comfortable talking about any and everything.

If you feel that you can talk about anything without feeling judged or belittled in any way, this is also a good sign. Successful marriages usually have this in common: the couple has a sense of liberty to share their feelings in a loving and safe environment, knowing they will be heard and respected for doing so. The fact is that you are both individuals with your own thoughts and opinions, so you won't always see eye to eye on everything. However, as long as you are able to discuss your feelings openly and honestly, and come to an agreement, it means that you are dealing with an understanding and mature person. Maturity and understanding are character traits that you DO NOT want to compromise on when considering a mate. If the person you're getting to know has them both, fantastic! Remain prayerful and continue to get to know him/her.

5. Are you attracted to the person?

If you experience attraction at first sight, fantastic. If not, don't worry too much about it, this does not mean they cannot be a potential courter. After interviewing a few married women on my blog (www.singlereadywaiting.blogspot.com) on the topic of "How Did You Meet Your Mate," some admitted to not having any attraction at first, but it came after they took the time to get to know each other. Therefore, don't be too quick to write someone off when you don't experience that initial attraction. When God is in it, like some of these women said, the attraction will come; it's only a matter of time.

Why 3 years as the maximum amount of time to be in a relationship?

In the Bible the number three is very significant. Besides being the number of manifestation, it is mentioned numerous times throughout scripture to establish God's will and His purpose. Here are a few examples:

✓Jesus died and rose on the 3rd day (1 Corinthians 15:4).

✓Jesus was tempted 3 times (Matthew 4:10).

✓Jesus prayed in the garden 3 times (Matthew 26).

✓Jesus asked Peter 3 times if He loved Him and to feed His sheep (John 21:15).

✓Jonah in the belly of the fish for 3 days and 3 nights (Matthew 12:40).

✓God used Wendy to call me three days before leaving town to bring about my deliverance.

✓And Robert and Tanika got married in the 3rd year of their courtship. (We may not be written in the Bible, but we were definitely a match made in heaven.)

We were able to build a solid friendship, enjoy our courtship and walk confidently down the aisle knowing that God brought us together. If you're not married within three years or less of being in a relationship with them, you should wonder why. If your desire is to be married and your relationship is beyond three years, seriously pray and ask God for His direction. You could be wasting your time with someone in a pothole.

Pothole #10—The Danger of Cohabitation

Times have changed and there is no doubt about that. In today's society, many people are choosing to live together rather than wait until marriage. They feel that in order to know a person well, and be completely sure that he/she is the one for him/her, they have to live together first.

Some of the dangers of living together are:

• Fornication. The chances of remaining chaste until marriage while living together is next to impossible (if you think you can, you don't know your flesh). The Scripture clearly says in I Corinthains 6:13, *"Now the body is not for fornication."* So, ladies and gents, please take all necessary precautions to avoid this from happening.

- Legal ramifications. If an unmarried couple purchases a property and the relationship breaks down, significant problems regarding issues of ownership could arise, this may then result in an unnecessary lengthy litigation.

- Your temporary situation of trying to figure out if you want to marry him/her may become a permanent situation if/when a baby comes into the picture. The danger: You may feel forced to marry, because of the child. Or, you could end up leaving this relationship after realizing he/she is not the one.

- Lose conviction of entering into a legal marriage and settle for a common-law marriage instead. Of course a common-law marriage requires neither a license nor a wedding, so the commitment of staying together, is either very slim or non-existent. The danger is that your children could grow up losing respect for you, the Church and the things of God, and if you desire to marry, you may never end up marrying at all. This of course would be very disappointing especially for you ladies, because I know from everyday experiences that most ladies want to get married. I see the joy, the excitement and delight that radiates from the newly engaged lady, as she talks to family and friends, and starts planning her wedding. I will also venture to say that even some men are quite delighted for this event as well; I know that my husband was. So, our God in all his wisdom, knew what was best for us, and how happy it could make us, when He instituted marriage (the legal one).

What is the alternative?

Well the last time I checked I didn't recall seeing courtship with benefits in the Bible. So look at it this way if you waited as long as you have to meet Mr./Mrs. Right, how much can it hurt to wait a bit longer, until you say "I do," then move in together? If you are both serious about each other, then you should show your love and respect for each other and... "wait." Ladies if your man is the aggressor in this case, then you should remind yourselves that you are worth waiting for! This is not one of those times to compromise...so Don't! When all is said and done, you both will be happy that you waited! Everything will be so much more beautiful!

Are You Truly Waiting?

Now that you are aware of what to look out for, you can proceed onto the highway.

It's exciting to know that you're truly single and ready. This is exactly where God wants you to be when he presents Mr. or Miss Right. But before their arrival you have to pass this inevitable STOP: "Waiting." How someone responds at this STOP often depends on the following factors:

✓Age

✓How long one has been truly single and ready

✓One's desire to be married

While the majority of singles desire to be married, there are some who don't wish to marry at all. No matter what category you find yourself in, the truth is this, if you're not waiting for a mate, could you be waiting for something else?

A week before writing this STOP I experienced overwhelming feelings of frustration and sadness. I was waiting on God to bring something to pass in my own life and it hadn't happened (yet). I don't believe it was a coincidence that I felt this way. God allowed me to be reacquainted with the feelings I experienced as a single to better relate to those of you who may be feeling this way right now. As a single, I had days when I thought, "What about me?" Then I would break out into singing "Pass Me Not O Gentle Saviour," an oldie but goodie hymn. Kidding aside, if we are not careful in this season of waiting, it could literally steal our joy and cause us to lose interest in going to church or spending time with friends and family. How then should we handle the wait? Don't throw pity parties!

When I decided to stop hosting pity parties, I lost some friends. Some of them you probably already know. They were: frustration, anger, resentment, bitterness and sadness. They don't come around as often as they used to; all because I chose not to entertain and make them feel at home. I figured I was either going to trust God and have a positive attitude while I wait, or not trust God and have a negative attitude while waiting. I chose option one.

SRW Words of Caution:

Where there is anger or frustration because of uncontrollable situations in life, we sometimes end up taking matters into our own hands to gain a sense of control. This is where the temptation to step outside of God's known will could take place.

For example:

- Choosing to court an unbeliever.
- Women pursuing men.
- Courting someone that God says not to.

Where does your anger or frustration lead you? What did Joseph do?

If there was anyone that had all the right reasons to be angry and host the biggest pity party ever, it would have been Joseph. He was sold by his brothers and put into prison after being falsely accused (see Genesis 39:13–23). Rather than taking revenge, Joseph kept the faith and a positive attitude. He served Potiphar faithfully with diligence and integrity (Genesis 39:1–6) and was later elevated second to Pharaoh in power (Genesis 41:37–57). God rewards those who are faithful!

Interesting things could happen while you wait.

I had my wedding dress hidden in my closet for four years before I ever met my husband. If this sounds weird to you, how I got the dress will seem even more weird. During the time that I was off-again with Peter, the Holy Spirit told me to go to a certain department store because my wedding dress was waiting for me. How weird and confusing was that? The Bible says to try the spirit to see if it is of God, so I went to the department store. I got to the dress department and there it was—a beautiful white dress, just waiting for me in the right size and with an amazing price. I tried it on and everyone in the change room commented on how beautiful the dress was, how blessed I was to find it, and that it looked like a wedding dress. "If this dress was not for my marriage to Peter, (because in my heart I was not sure about marrying him) who was it for?" I wondered alone in the change room. In 2009, this was the dress that I wore on my wedding day when I married Robert. It was the best $124.00 I ever spent. (Want to see this dress? Visit my website www.singlereadyandwaiting.com.) When you follow the leading of the Holy Spirit you can never go wrong. God will take care of you!

Remember to Live While Waiting

I.L.V.E. (pronounced I Live)

I—Invest in you.

There are so many ways that you can invest in yourself. For some:

✓Taking that much needed trip to rejuvenate.

✓Attend a business seminar to get fresh ideas for your business.

✓Start budgeting to pay off debt.

✓Or find a good Christian counselor?

Do you feel like your life has been going in circles? Have you been making wrong decisions? Do you have difficulty trusting? Are you living in fear? Do you feel unloved? Or, are you trying to be what others think you should be? Then I encourage you to do as I did, invest in yourself by finding a Spirit-filled Christian counselor. It was the best investment I ever made.

After my courtship collision, I knew that I needed to heal from that relationship and deal with the past hurts and disappointments that I held inside. It was my way of taking back the control that I felt I lost along the way. Through the Christian counselor I was able to pinpoint the unhealthy cycles I was repeating in my own life, and how I could break free from them.

The Investment Payout I Didn't See Coming

The day that I had my first appointment with Rev. Brown, I met my future husband. He and I got to the front doors of the Christian College at the same time. I opened the door for him because his hands were full with musical instruments. We both waited for the elevator to come and then went inside. We learned each other's name, and he asked what church I attended and that was it. But, as God's divine providence would have it that was not my last encounter with Robert. When I was truly READY and WAITING, God allowed us to meet again at the appointed time nine months later. You shall be positioned at the right place and at the right time to meet your mate in Jesus' name!

L—Love God and the people around you.

Never allow the wait to steal your joy. Take the time you have now to be intimate with God and spend quality time with your family and friends.

V—Volunteer your time, skills and/or gifts (at schools, organizations, place of worship, etc.).

Everyone's got something to offer. Share your wisdom and knowledge in the area you are most passionate about.

E—Exercise and eat healthy

It's important to take care of ourselves by staying in shape and eating healthy.

I am not a health expert, but after spending enough time reading health books and magazines, I know that healthy eating is the way to keep our bodies in peak condition. Therefore, the type of food we eat and the exercise we do, will impact our overall health. *"For bodily exercise profiteth little: but godliness is profitable unto all things, having promise of the life that now is, and of that which is to come"* (1 Timothy 4:8).

83

If I Join an On-Line Dating Site Does This Mean I'm Not Waiting?

There is no denying that times have changed. Friends and relatives are not trying to match their single friends like they used to, making online dating favourable to some. No, it does not mean that you are not waiting if you join a dating site. However, you would not be waiting if you do not have a sense of peace in your spirit about joining the site, and ended up joining anyway. This could be the Holy Spirit telling you to wait. He has other plans. If there is peace in joining a Christian site, then the decision is yours. But as your guide I got to tell you, not everyone that says they are a Christian, "tall, dark and handsome" is Christian, tall, dark and handsome. BEWARE.

Whether you meet someone online or offline, my answer is the same, you are not truly waiting unless you are truly "Single and Ready" first. If you are, remember to keep your standards, follow the "SRW Signals" and remain prayerful about any men/women you meet.

Adjust to "The Wait"

Like the four seasons: spring, summer, fall and winter, we have no control over how long or short the wait will be. Nature just takes its course and we adjust to the changing weather. In the winter, we adjust by getting winter or all season tires, and in the summer, we adjust to the heat by purchasing a windshield sunshade to prevent the sun from beating on the dashboard and steering wheel. So it is with the season of waiting. The only difference is that this adjustment is an internal one. In order to pass through this STOP, we need to feed our minds with God's word to ward off any thoughts that may try to take us off the path God has us on. Honestly, only God knows why some meet their mate sooner than others so in the meantime learn to rejoice with those who receive a mate after waiting and be encouraged to know that God is faithful to those who put their trust in Him.

STOP 8

Let's Talk About Sex

"No Wed, No Bed" these are the words I saw one day as I was searching through YouTube. Then I bumped into another title that said "80% of Christians Having Sex."

Why are so many Christians not waiting until their wedding day?

If God's Word is not a weighty enough reason to wait, what is?

These are just some of the questions that came to mind. Then I wrote a list of reasons why Christians engage in sex before marriage.

Some reasons are:

- Their flesh is in control.

- Peer pressure.

- They place themselves in uncompromising situations.

- They feel it is okay to have sex with someone they plan on marrying.

- To keep someone interested in them.

- To have a child because their biological clock is ticking.

• To please someone else.

After my relationship with Peter came to an end, I was determined to make wiser decisions. This time I would choose to please God more than giving in to my flesh or someone else's.

The Wise Choice to Wait

Though not popular, the benefits for waiting are well worth it!

When I walked down the aisle of my church that sunny day in September tears filled my eyes. The love that Robert and I had for each other, and our dedication to God in choosing to remain chaste, made our wedding day that more special. We may not have been virgins (this would have been better), but the moment we entered a courting relationship we made the decision to do things God's way. The same decision we have to make every day in our Christian walk.

Be Encouraged

If you are a virgin, take that detour and avoid compromising situations that may put your virginity at risk. It is a gift from God and should be treasured. If you have had sex in the past, be encouraged. Know that "*There is therefore now no condemnation to them which are in Christ Jesus, who walk not after the flesh, but after the Spirit*" (Romans 8:1). So, ask God for forgiveness it will be given. "*If we confess our sins, he is faithful and just and will forgive us our sins and purify us from all unrighteousness*" (1 John 1:9 NIV). Now, like Jesus said to the woman caught in adultery, "*Go, and sin no more*" (John 8:11).

Biblical Story of the Woman Caught in Adultery

The teachers of the law and the Pharisees brought in a woman caught in adultery. They made her stand before the group and said to Jesus, *"Teacher, this woman was caught in the act of adultery. In the Law Moses commanded us to stone such women. Now what do you say?" They were using this question as a trap, in order to have a basis for accusing him. But Jesus bent down and started to write on the ground with his finger. When they kept on questioning him, he straightened up and said to them, "If any one of you is without sin, let him be the first to throw a stone at her." Again he stooped down and wrote on the ground. At this, those who heard began to go away one at a time, the older ones first, until only Jesus was left, with the woman still standing there. Jesus straightened up and asked her, "Woman, where are they? Has no one condemned you?" "No one, sir," she said. Then neither do I condemn you," Jesus declared. "Go now and leave your life of sin"* (John 8:3–11 NIV).

9 Types of Men You Should Think Twice About Courting

The types of men I am about to describe are single men that can be ready but just aren't there yet. These are nine types of men you've probably already met or will meet that you should think twice about entering a courting relationship with. Though these nine are about men, women can be these types too, as I was the "Double-minded" woman for years, and Peter was the "Just Got Saved Man." The key to this STOP is to recognize if you are one of them, or have met someone who is. No one wants to waste years in a relationship that is going nowhere.

1. I Might Be Grown But I'm Still a Boy Man

You know the ones that don't seem to grow up and don't quite comprehend 1 Corinthians 13:11 (NIV), "*When I was a child, I talked like a child, I thought like a child, I reasoned like a child. When I became a man, I put childish ways behind me.*" You shouldn't hold your breath on this one. The best thing to do if you meet a man like this is to tell him the truth. Remember, in the Lord we are all sisters and brothers first before we become anything more. Don't talk behind his/her back, let them know about their childish ways, in a tactful way of course, and who knows, they may snap out of it, and get prepared for the one they will meet later down the road.

2. Just Got Saved Man

It is best that a new convert spends alone time with God to grow and know Him intimately without any distraction. If you would be more of a distraction than someone that could help him in his growth towards spiritual maturity, step away and allow God to mold him into the man he has called him to be. Remember he is your brother in the Lord, so pray that Christ be formed in him (Galatians 4:19). If he is for you it will happen. Relax, be a friend and leave the rest to God.

3. Not Financially Ready Man

Now, there is the man that says I cannot commit until I am financially ready. I personally agree with this man, but to a point. If he's talking about clearing up his student loan debt before making any commitments, depending on his income and other responsibilities, this could take a while. While your age can play a major factor in what you decide, know that commitment for these types of men may not come until they feel all their ducks are in a row. In this case you have two options: 1. Commit and wait it out. 2. Move on. If it's meant to be it will be; he's got your number.

4. I'm Fly and I Know that I'm a Fly Man

Now for the super fly, fine men who know how to put themselves together and just seem to smell good all the time. These types may have a hard time committing to a woman because maybe they are self-absorbed or just not interested in women all together. If this is not the case, most of these types of men still have a hard time committing, because they like to play the field and think they can get any woman they want. If this type of guy does not get a humble spirit and stay close to God, he just might remain single for the rest of his life. He is considered to be high risk to any woman. Words of caution: don't try to be superwoman and try to change him.

5. Super-Man

The guy that is mature but always thinks that he needs to save the world before he can commit to a relationship. He thinks a relationship will slow him down. For this man, he might just be called to a life of singleness? This would be absolutely fine. The worst thing you could do is force him into a committed relationship with you. Be a friend and nothing more. When he feels that he's finished conquering the world, he may give you a call.

6. The Must Have Sex Man

If a Christian man is pressuring you for sex, you ought to wonder why. Sex is a beautiful thing and God created it for our enjoyment within the confines of marriage. If waiting until marriage is important to you, and he is not willing to wait until that blessed day, then homey may not be the one for you. Ladies don't be fooled, a man can wait. A true man of God will want to wait with you; he has his own fear of God and a desire to please Him.

7. I'm Still Hurt Man

This type of man is hurt because he hasn't really gotten over the painful breakup with his ex. Relationships can really make or break you. All it takes is a bad relationship and it can steal years away from your life trying to get healed from it. This is why it is so important that you take your time getting to know someone and be very prayerful. While he is making an attempt to move on with you, he's having a hard time moving forward. He's afraid to commit in fear of getting hurt again. For this type of man, time and much prayer is needed. Pray for him and when he's ready, hopefully you'll still be around.

8. The Double-Minded Man

Today he is sure about you, but tomorrow he's not. Fear and doubt are usually the main reasons why a man may be double-minded. It would be important for this man to take a closer look at his fears and doubts. Could it be a fear of commitment? I would suggest not getting into a committed relationship with him until he is completely sure of what he wants, or else it will be a roller coaster ride for you. Keep your distance and pray that he will receive the clarity he needs to make a final decision.

9. Not Responsible and Accountable Man

- He doesn't take responsibility for his actions and plays the blame game.

- He doesn't think about the consequences of his actions before he does it.

- He doesn't pay his bills on time.

- He doesn't do what he says he's going to do 95 percent of the time.

- He isn't reliable and dependable.

- He only cares about himself and is not a positive example to other men.

- He neglects the needs of his own home.

- He cannot be trusted.

- He is not honest with himself and makes excuses.

- He doesn't pray or spend any time with God or His Word.

- He is not a good steward of his finances.

- He says I LOVE YOU and doesn't mean it.

- He is not looking for a commitment.

If a man falls within this category, hope is not completely lost for him. Be a friend and pray that he will become the responsible and accountable kind of man he needs to be. God works in mysterious ways; who knows, this frog could end up being your prince one day.

SRW Accountable and Responsible Man Checklist

(This one's a keeper…just the opposite of the above.)

✓He takes responsibility for his actions and doesn't play the blame game.

✓He thinks about the consequences of his actions before he does it.

✓He pays his bills on time.

✓He does what he says he is going to do 95 percent of the time.

✓He is reliable and dependable.

✓He doesn't only care about himself, he wants to be a positive example to other men.

✓He cares about the needs of his own home.

✓He can be trusted.

✓He is honest with himself and doesn't give excuses.

✓He spends regular time with God in prayer and reading His Word.

✓He is a good steward of his finances.

✓He doesn't say the words I LOVE YOU unless he means it.

✓He is looking for a commitment.

In closing, never enter a courting relationship blindly: be alert and aware of the type of people you meet and take Maya Angelou's advice "The first time someone shows you who they are, believe them." Then decide if you're still interested in getting into their car. "*Wait on the LORD: be of good courage, and he shall strengthen thine heart: wait, I say, on the LORD*" (Psalm 27:14).

How to Attract Marriage-Minded Men into the Church

The best way to attract marriage-minded men into the church is to simply be a God-fearing woman.

I will never forget a day in October 2011 when I accompanied my husband to an event. He went to park the car and I stood by the venue waiting for his return. As I waited, I couldn't help but notice a gentleman walking by with a confused look on his face, almost like he wasn't sure where he was going. So I asked if he was looking for the same event we were going to and he said yes, with a sigh of relief. Robert arrived and I introduced them.

We stood in line together and talked about different subjects. Then I popped my SRW questions (it was only a matter of time).

✓Are you single?

✓Are you ready?

✓Are you waiting?

He laughed hysterically and asked if I was joking. I took out my business card to show how serious I was and he laughed some more. Robert, the team player that he is, went on about the SRW initiative and how he was proud of me for starting it. I told our new friend that it is also a Christian singles group. This is when he felt led to tell us about the Christian ladies he met, while in church. He used to be a regular attendee but he walked away from church and God. He also went on to say that the Christian women he encountered were not very different from the women he dated outside of the church. This was also a turn off for him from the church.

As you could imagine, this was very disturbing to hear. Although I believe that Christians should not walk away from the church or God because of what others do or say, if a person is weak in his/her faith, or is a new Christian, a bad witness can cause that one to stumble. It was hard to hear this, but it could very well be the truth for more men in and outside of our churches today.

What I Learned From My Blood Brothers

Having grown up with brothers, I always heard about two types of women and two types of men.

The two types of women are: "**Girlfriend Material**" and "**Wifey Material**." The difference between the two is the mindset. Those that fell within the "Girlfriend Material" were usually immature women who had been sexually active with many men. The "Wifey Material" was mature women who had respect for themselves and their bodies and were not promiscuous in any way.

The two types of men are: "**The Player**" and "**The Good Guy**."

"The Player" is a man who tries to be Mr. Right to more than one woman while being sexually active with them.

"The Good Guy" is a "one woman man."

What Kind of Material are You?

There was a time when men went to church to find a "good woman." But this is changing. They are no longer looking inside the church to find one. Could it be that Christian women have lowered their standards, or maybe didn't have a standard to begin with? Or does a woman feel that in order to keep a man she has to be willing to "give out something?" Whatever the reason, it's time that the church be the church and take back what the enemy might have stolen: holiness, value and integrity.

How Can We Help to Change This?

"*Let your light so shine before* **men**, *that they may see your good works, and glorify your Father which is in heaven*" (Matthew 5:16, emphasis added). This means one sister at a time.

As Christian women, we need to be a Godly example to our fellow sisters and brothers in and outside of the church. If this means making wiser decisions about where to go with a man to avoid compromising situations, then do so. Even if you think you are strong enough to be alone with a man without engaging in sex, this may not be the case for him. You may want to please God by waiting and he may not have this same desire. Therefore, don't take chances you may end up regretting.

Be A Wise Woman

Being a light that shines before men is not only about keeping yourself sexually, but it is also the love and devotion you have for God that comes out in the way you speak, dress and conduct yourself. Any woman that has a pretty face and a great body can get a man to look in her direction, but only a wise woman can really get their attention.

When Joab needed a particular assignment to be done He sent someone to the country of Tekoa to get him a "*wise*" woman (2 Samuel 14:2). Ladies, when a man is ready for a wise woman He will recognize you as one. They know the difference.

So How Do We Get More Marriage-Minded Men into the Church?

✓Be a God-fearing woman with integrity. Love God with your whole heart, mind, and soul. The men will respect you more and consider you to be "Wifey Material."

✓Choose to be a positive witness to the men you meet, Christian and non-Christian, knowing that they are souls that can be won for Christ. Pay close attention to the way you speak, dress and conduct yourself in their presence.

✓Invite them to church. They may or may not show up but at least you've given them an invitation. Who knows, one day when you least expect it, he may surprise you.

✓Be a wise woman. "*If any of you lack wisdom, let him ask of God, that giveth to all men liberally, and upbraideth not; and it shall be given him*" (James 1:5).

Daughters of Zion, God is counting on you to be the holy example He has called you to be for the world and church to see.

The Transition

This is the final stop before courtship. The number eleven (11) represents the following

1. Two truly single, ready and waiting individuals.

2. The last hour on the clock before a new day.

The new day is the "Sacred Stage of Courtship." This is the stage where you can emotionally express your feelings and allow your love to blossom towards engagement. You couldn't express them freely in the "friendship stage" but now you can. What a relief! However, before you can get there you have to pass through "The Transition."

"The Transition" is the period between the "Friendship Stage" and the next level which is "The Sacred Stage of Courtship." In this transitional period, the person decides that he/she knows enough about the other person and is ready to take their friendship to the next level. To paint a much clearer picture of this, here are some examples:

Scenario #1

Jimmy and Sue are friends and have been getting to know each other mostly over the phone for the past three months. They've talked about their values, future goals, what they have in common, etc. They enjoyed their conversations together and made plans to see each other more often. It's now six months and they feel inseparable.

"The Transition"

Jimmy: (He knows she is marriage material and since he is looking for a wife he wants to start seeing her exclusively). Sue, I just love being with you... and... would like to begin courting you. How do you feel about that?

Scenario #2

Mike and Sandra have been friends for one year. They prefer to have face-to-face interaction, rather than speaking over the phone. They met at coffee shops, attended group gatherings and went out for dinners. Sandra has been patient with Mike but lately she has been wondering where their friendship is going. Both have expressed that they have prayed about the direction of their friendship, but never had a conversation about it. Therefore, Sandra being the assertive woman that she is took the risk of asking Mike a serious question during a walk in the park.

"The Transition"

Sandra: Mike, I have been really enjoying our conversations very much and I hope it never ends. It has been a year and I have been praying about us for some time. I value our friendship, but lately my feelings have been growing stronger for you.

Mike: I am so happy you brought this up. I have been thinking and praying about us for some time as well and the last thing I want you to feel is that I've been stringing you along. I have been taking my time in getting to know you, because I wanted to build a solid friendship first before taking it to another level. I like everything about you and I think this time is good as any to let you know that I'm interested in courting you.

As you can see from these scenarios, there isn't a "Transition" without first having a serious conversation about one's true feelings for the other person. If a meaningful relationship that leads to marriage is what you are looking for, then don't be afraid to express this when you are ready. Ladies, I would suggest that you give the man the opportunity to take the initiative in this area, but if you feel like Sandra in the above scenario, taking the risk could work in your favour. It will not scare off the truly Single and Ready man that is looking for who you are and what you have to offer: courtship. Never forget that "The Transition" to a courting relationship is always marked by a conversation; so be sure to look out for this.

To make a wise "Transition," it is extremely important to know the right information about the person. No major decision is worth making without first asking the right questions and acknowledging God.

When I was getting to know Robert, a friend told me about a new book from a prominent preacher, and that it had twenty questions in it that people should ask themselves before making a serious commitment. I took her suggestion and asked if Robert would like to visit a major bookstore with me. It was so funny; there we were sitting side by side holding this book and reading question number one. We stopped at question number three and decided to go back to finish the rest another time. Some stores allow you to read a portion of a book before purchasing it. We never did make it back, God had other plans.

About a month after our book store visit, I woke up with a strong leading to sit at my computer. This is when the Holy Spirit began giving me questions for Robert and me. Without counting, I typed everything I heard and immediately called Robert to let him know what happened. "Robert, you won't believe what happened this morning. The Holy Spirit gave me questions and I am convinced they are for us." I said.

"How many?" He replied. After counting them I was in awe; there were twenty. This could have been the reason we never did make it back to the store or why we just didn't purchase the book all together. God had a master plan with our names on it!

The Assignment

The assignment was to send Robert the questions and we would answer and forward our answers to each other via e-mail at the same time. The purpose for this was to learn as much as possible about each other to know if we were compatible suitors to begin with. "*Can two walk together, except they be agreed?*" (Amos 3:3). We found out that we agreed on 90% of our answers. (If you are interested in receiving a copy of these "Twenty Questions," please visit www.singlereadyandwaiting.com.)

As you consider someone for courtship, be sure to focus on what matters most. This is where so many singles turn away potential suitors and don't enter a courting relationship, let alone walk down the aisle. When I made a list of what I was looking for in a mate, I left room for my friend Grace.

My Dear Friend Grace

Grace is a very kind and forgiving friend. There are many times when we make certain poor decisions or commit some really bad actions that are deserving of punishment and perhaps even being cut off. Yet, "Grace" stands in the gap by giving us a second and even a third chance to do or make things right. Do you know that one friend who you can always count on? Well, this is Grace. She always sees our potential and won't be too quick to write us off. Do you have a list that details the kind of person you would like to have as your mate? If so, Grace may ask you to be more accommodating, forgiving or accepting of a certain individual who could be your perfect match. I was not interested in marrying a man who was divorced and Robert was not interested in marrying a non-virgin. However, God had other plans. Had it not been for "SRW Signal #7" and Grace, we probably would never have given each other a fair chance. Today, I am so glad that I listened to Grace. So, while you are on your journey towards courtship, my suggestion is for you to write a list of things that you are looking for in your mate, and you may just get what you are asking for (Robert and I got 80% of what we believed God for). It will be absolutely awesome if you find a mate who matches your list 100%. However, it is important that you do not allow this list to override the SRW Signal #7 and/or Grace, which are in place to assist you in not missing out on God's very best for you. This means there is a possibility that your future mate may not match your list 100%, and you may have to ask your friend Grace to assist you in either forgiving or accepting him/her for the balance. After all, the list will be your desires that will not always line up with God's will for you 100%, and because God knows you better than yourself. He should have the final say in helping you to find the right mate. Just do your part and allow Him to do the rest!

"Sacred Stage of Courtship"

Only a few paragraphs away from allowing your love to blossom even more for the person God has given His green light to. However, before you get there you have to know what makes this stage a sacred one. God has led you to the right person to enter a courting relationship with. Now it's all about timing. Please understand this, the "Sacred Stage of Courtship" should be a brief STOP, one to two years, which is the recommended maximum amount of time you should spend before getting engaged. Then spend the rest of your life getting to know each other.

Our "Transition"—Not Quite There Yet...Wait

When Robert asked to court me, though I felt he was the one, and wanted to accept his request, I wanted to still pray and fast to hear what the Lord was saying (I was not going to make the same mistakes twice). No matter how many green lights there are, rushing into a relationship is never the right thing to do. Prior to us meeting, Robert told me he prayed and fasted for a wife and when we met he was 100% sure, this time, that I was the one. He was prepared to go right into courting. Nevertheless he joined in on the fast. The answer I got from God after praying and waiting for it was to continue building a friendship. The answer Robert got came in the form of a dream.

Robert's Dream

He dreamt that we were driving about 100 km, smooth sailing, and then suddenly something supernaturally slammed on the brakes and slowed us right down to about 20 km hour. In the dream, Robert wondered why we were slowing down so drastically. Then, not long after, a big tractor trailer went by, tipped over and fell on all the cars in front of us. Robert then realized why there was a drastic brake. The same God that told me "continue to build a friendship" was the same God that slammed on the brakes in Robert's dream. We remained friends for another six months before I was given the green light to make "The Transition." Clearly, waiting is not only something you do before Mr. Right comes along, you may be required to wait even when the right person is in view. God knows best. Allow Him to guide you through every stage, especially "The Transition." Now I can hear you saying, "are we there yet?" as we make the final approach towards to the final STOP. My response is: "not until you turn the page."

 **STOP 12**

Sacred Stage of Courtship

You have arrived! Welcome to courtship! Love is in the air and you are ready to develop a deeper relationship. You should be thrilled that the search could very well be over and you are with someone that is worthy of you and your time. I hope you are experiencing great peace as this is what comes along with being with the right person.

Although the word *courtship* is not in the Bible, its meaning is sacred because it has been proven to succeed in biblical times. When something is sacred it is "worthy of spiritual respect or devotion and can be ascribed to people, objects or times." Your courtship will be a sacred one but this depends on you. God has given us the power to decree a thing and it will be established in our lives. "*Thou shalt also decree a thing, and it shall be established unto thee: and the light shall shine upon thy ways*" (Job 22:28). If you desire to have a successful and sacred courtship as a truly single, ready and waiting person, begin to pray what you want to see. Pray that the following components exist in your relationship:

1. Two people who desire to please God at all times
2. Two people who are teachable and have a desire to grow

3. Two people who understand they are building a solid foundation for marriage in their courtship, i.e. they are praying and reading God's Word together and privately. They have mutual respect for each other; an open and honest form of communication, while understanding and learning how to care and support one another during the quality time they spend together.

4. Revering each other's body as the temple of God. Abstaining from fornication.

5. Accountability. A pastor/parent has met your courter and approves of your courting relationship.

6. Conflict and disagreements. You and your courter are able to solve conflicts and come to a resolve. (Being able to solve problems in the courtship stage will prepare you for the marriage.)

Once these factors are evident in your courting relationship, you are off to a great start. God is with you and before you know it, you will be saying YES and letting everyone know about the proposal.

What I Remember and What You Need to Know

During my courtship, I remember learning and growing so much over the year and six months. The challenges that came our way allowed us to develop the God kind of love we now have for each other. Agape love: to love unconditionally is an essential element for a successful marriage. Without it, I'm telling you a marriage would not thrive! In your courtship, be sure to experience this kind of love along with acceptance of one another.

Now, although you are with the right person, don't forget that he/she is not perfect. Like you, he/she has strengths and weaknesses, and by the time you get to courtship you should have seen what they are. This is why you don't speed into a relationship. I know, by now I sound like a broken record, but this is one record you don't want to pawn. It is the key to avoiding accidents and collisions. Improve on being a better you and don't be too critical of each other. Instead, make a chart (here comes another assignment) and write down your weaknesses and strengths. You should see that he/she is strong where you are weak. Then focus on their strengths and positive qualities, and they yours. Don't forget, time spent in your presence should always be a positive one. He/she needs to see why coming home to you everyday is worth it.

What to Do with Concerns in Courtship

If you are having some concerns, don't be alarmed, this is normal. It does not mean you are with the wrong person. Through prayer the Holy Spirit could give you practical things to do that can remedy the concern. It happened for us. As long as God is the author of your coming together, there is nothing you both cannot overcome. They say practice makes perfect, so practice going to God in prayer about any, and everything from now. If you do, this practice will continue in marriage; another good quality for successful Christian marriages.

Family

While in the stage of courtship it is a great time to introduce him/her to your family. Remember, if your parent(s) approval of the person you are in courtship with, is important to you, then the sooner you do so (in this stage) the better. During my courtship, Robert took my mother and I out for dinner. This was his way of breaking the ice and letting her know that he was very serious about me. I didn't have to ask my mom (aka sweet "M's") if she liked him or didn't like him. Their conversation just flowed and she had a pleasant smile on her face, so I knew right away that she did.

We all hope that our parents, family, and friends will like the one courting us as much as we do, but this is not always the case. There are happily married couples today that don't necessarily get along with their in-laws for various reasons. This does not mean that they were not the right choice for each other; nor will it mean that for you either, if you find yourself in that situation. As long as God is the author of your courtship, which I believe He will be after following everything so far in this book, they will hopefully come around to accepting him/her.

Friends

When it comes to introducing your courter to other family members and friends, I would suggest that you use your discretion. Not everyone who says, "I am happy that you've met someone," is genuinely happy for you because remember, misery loves company. With that being said, you should be very selective about who you share information with. This is especially vital should you happen to hit a bump on the courtship road. The right friends will give you feedback to help strengthen your relationship rather than try to break it up. They will offer to pray with you, and give you sound advice. To this very day, I am so thankful for the way God used a neighbour of mine. She always gave me a listening ear when I knocked on her door. Then I would leave refreshed by the wisdom and sound advice she would give me. It helped my relationship for the better. Once again, if God is the author of your coming together, He will strategically place the right people into your path. He did it for me, so He will most certainly do it for you too.

Although You Are With The Right Person, Don't Lose Yourself

While you are learning more and more about each other, do not lose your identity to this person. Continue to have a life. Never assume or make the decision to put your life, dreams or plans on hold, in order to fully invest in your courting and eventual marriage relationship. The right person will be a compliment to you, supporting you in your endeavours, rather than being a hindrance to them. (This is not to say that they will agree with everything you do. Also, when you are married, there may be times when you may have to compromise with some things in order to keep the peace of God in your home.) Continue to take time out for your family, friends and the hobbies that you love. (i.e. writing, playing sports, music etc.) If you stop pursuing the things that are important to you, regret can set in, as well as resentment toward your courter. I.L.V.E. does not stop once you enter the "Sacred Stage of Courtship," it continues. Only this time you will have company.

Don't Forget About the Purpose of this "Sacred Stage"

While you are having fun time will fly by, so don't forget the purpose of courtship. Remember this is a brief STOP towards engagement. Continue to build a solid foundation and then proceed to engagement.

There is so much more to share about this exciting "Sacred Stage of Courtship," but I will have to leave it here. Should you want to know how to navigate successfully through courtship, engagement and then marriage, read our book *Love, It's Worth the Weight: You Two Can Have a Love Story* written by my husband, Robert, and me.

CONCLUSION

As your guide, it has been my pleasure to share my experience down this road with you. It is my prayer that you will consider taking the road less travelled. Dating is the popular thing to do, and it has also convinced those in the church of such; but not all. Some have chosen to wait and court. That's right, wait and court the right ONE that God has brought into your path. He has given His peace and you have His green light to enter a courting relationship with that ONE.

Contrary to popular belief, you don't have to date a number of men or women to figure this out. I don't only know this from personal experience, I know of many people that have gone out on multiple dates and still felt he/she was not the right person. Sure, they may have gained experience, but will this experience make the relationship with the right courter any better? No; spending time to become truly single, ready and waiting and building memories, only with the right one is much better.

Ladies and gents you must trust God with this area of your life. If He knows the number of hairs that is on your head he must know who would be your perfect match. If you choose to consider a match making service, be very sure that it's God guiding you and not a decision made out of desperation.

Friendship First

Remember, before anything, build a solid foundation as friends first using the "SRW Hands-off Approach." It will help to guard your heart and not awaken love before the right time. Take it slow and allow one's true character to be seen. As friends, pay close attention to how you spend time getting to know each other. You want to avoid late night home visits like the plague. Instead, get to know him/her over the phone or where people are around, e.g. a nearby coffee shop. Once you have gotten to know him/her and you have built a level of trust, then you may take him up on his offer to attend a movie. In addition, I wouldn't advise that you pray together just yet. Pray on your own and ask God to reveal the purpose of your friendship.

In the Meantime

While you wait, declare: I.L.V.E. (I Live). Enjoy the life you have right now and be a holy example to everyone you meet. Your walk with Christ could literally bring someone closer to knowing Him, without ever saying a word.

"The Transition"

This is where most collisions occur. Do not speed in this lane; take it slow. Go into your prayer closet and wait for God's direction always. We can never go wrong in following Him.

Do you believe that God wants to write your love story? Well, He does more than you ever know. Keep trusting, believing, and walking hand in hand with Him until that day when He allows your paths to meet, and when it does I look forward to hearing all about your "Transition" story.

The "Sacred Stage of Courtship" is a STOP you don't want to overlook; especially if you are looking for a committed relationship that leads to marriage. By now everyone knows how to date and those that do, usually spend a lot of their valuable time, money and energy going on multiple dates with men/women who don't end up being their suitable match. This is not the case for those who choose to court. Instead of going on multiple dates they continue living out their life serving, trusting and waiting on God's perfect time to be presented with their future mate. As mentioned before, this STOP once entered, is a brief one. Therefore, be sure that you don't get stuck in a Pothole. However, if you do the option to see a Christian Counsellor is available to you.

What you also need to know at this stage is: don't misinterpret any concerns or misunderstandings you may have to mean your courter is not the one for you. Know that anything worth having is worth fighting for, especially when God is in it. Do the work now and position yourself for a marriage that will be off to a great start.

Looks like we've come to the end of our road and it's time to say goodbye. I hope you were encouraged, enlightened and helped by the information shared, as it was my pleasure being your road guide. Until we meet again, may the greatest guide of all continue to sustain you, as you place your future into His capable hands.

Soul-Tie PRAYER AND SCRIPTURES THAT HELPED GUIDE ME WHEN I WAS SINGLE

Soul-Tie Prayer

Father God, I thank you for saving me from destruction. I praise you for sending Jesus to die for my sins. Please forgive me for my sins against you. Specifically, I confess that I _____ (details of the sin and names). I repent of that sin and renounce it now. Lord, please purify my heart from this sin, the memory of it and any associated fantasy I have entertained in my mind regarding it. In the name of Jesus Christ and by the power of his blood shed on the cross, I cut myself free from any soul-ties that may have been established with _____ (names or specific objects). I commit him/her/them to the care of Jesus Christ for him to do with as He wills. Satan, I rebuke you in all your works and ways. I rebuke any evil spirits that have a foothold in me. In the name of Jesus, I command you evil spirits to leave me and go directly to Jesus Christ. Father, please heal my soul of any wounds resulting from these soul-ties. Please reintegrate any part of me that may have been detained through this/these soul-ties and restore me to wholeness. I also ask that you will reintegrate any part of the person(s) I sinned with that has been detained in me, and restore them to wholeness. Thank you, Lord, for your healing power and your perfect love for me. May I glorify you with my life from this point forward. In Jesus' name, Amen.

More on soul-ties here:
http://healingprayer.wordpress.com/soul-ties.

Scriptures

For the LORD God is a sun and shield: the LORD will give grace and glory: no good thing will he withhold from them that walk uprightly (Psalm 84:11).

In all thy ways acknowledge him, and he shall direct thy paths (Proverbs 3:6).

For I know the thoughts that I think toward you, saith the LORD, thoughts of peace, and not of evil, to give you an expected end (Jeremiah 29:11).

Come unto me, all ye that labour and are heavy laden, and I will give you rest (Matthew 11:28).

And he said unto me, My grace is sufficient for thee: for my strength is made perfect in weakness. Most gladly therefore will I rather glory in my infirmities, that the power of Christ may rest upon me (2 Corinthians 12:9).

Wait on the LORD: be of good courage, and he shall strengthen thine heart: wait, I say, on the LORD (Psalm 27:14).

And prepare yourselves by the houses of your fathers, after your courses, according to the writing of David king of Israel, and according to the writing of Solomon his son (2 Chronicles 35:4).

Behold, I will do a new thing; now it shall spring forth; shall ye not know it? I will even make a way in the wilderness, and rivers in the desert (Isaiah 43:19).

Therefore if any man be in Christ, he is a new creature: old things are passed away; behold, all things are become new (2 Corinthians 5:17).

Examine yourselves, whether ye be in the faith; prove your own selves. Know ye not your own selves, how that Jesus Christ is in you, except ye be reprobates? (2 Corinthians 13:5).

And I will bring the blind by a way that they knew not; I will lead them in paths that they have not known: I will make darkness light before them, and crooked things straight. These things will I do unto them, and not forsake them (Isaiah 42:16).

Ask, and it shall be given you; seek, and ye shall find; knock, and it shall be opened unto you (Matthew 7:7).

Remember ye not the former things, neither consider the things of old (Isaiah 43:18).

Then said she, Sit still, my daughter, until thou know how the matter will fall: for the man will not be in rest, until he have finished the thing this day (Ruth 3:18).

Flee fornication. Every sin that a man doeth is without the body; but he that committeth fornication sinneth against his own body (1 Corinthians 6:18).

Likewise, ye younger, submit yourselves unto the elder. Yea, all of you be subject one to another, and be clothed with humility: for God resisteth the proud, and giveth grace to the humble (1 Peter 5:5).

Where no counsel is, the people fall: but in the multitude of counsellors there is safety (Proverbs 11:14).

Trust in the LORD with all thine heart; and lean not unto thine own understanding (Proverbs 3:5).

Some trust in chariots, and some in horses: but we will remember the name of the LORD our God (Psalm 20:7).

Now faith is the substance of things hoped for, the evidence of things not seen (Hebrews 11:1).

Not that I speak in respect of want: for I have learned, in whatsoever state I am, therewith to be content (Philippians 4:11).

But seek ye first the kingdom of God, and his righteousness; and all these things shall be added unto you (Matthew 6:33).

Flee also youthful lusts: but follow righteousness, faith, charity, peace, with them that call on the Lord out of a pure heart (2 Timothy 2:22).

If ye love me, keep my commandments (John 14:15).

To appoint unto them that mourn in Zion, to give unto them beauty for ashes, the oil of joy for mourning, the garment of praise for the spirit of heaviness; that they might be called trees of righteousness, the planting of the LORD, that he might be glorified (Isaiah 61:3).

I have been young, and now am old; yet have I not seen the righteous forsaken, nor his seed begging bread (Psalm 37:25).

For my yoke is easy, and my burden is light (Matthew 11:30).

I charge you, O daughters of Jerusalem, that ye stir not up, nor awake my love, until he please (Song of Solomon 8:4).

She said, No man, Lord. And Jesus said unto her, Neither do I condemn thee: go, and sin no more (John 8:11).

They that sow in tears shall reap in joy (Psalm 126:5).

Lift up your heads, O ye gates; and be ye lift up, ye everlasting doors; and the King of glory shall come in (Psalm 24:7).

With good will doing service, as to the Lord, and not to men: Knowing that whatsoever good thing any man doeth, the same shall he receive of the Lord, whether he be bond or free (Ephesians 6:7–8).

Serve the LORD with gladness: come before his presence with singing (Psalm 100:2).

I will instruct thee and teach thee in the way which thou shalt go: I will guide thee with mine eye (Psalm 32:8).

For the vision is yet for an appointed time, but at the end it shall speak, and not lie: though it tarry, wait for it; because it will surely come, it will not tarry (Habakkuk 2:3).

And the LORD answered me, and said, Write the vision, and make it plain upon tables, that he may run that readeth it (Habakkuk 2:2).

REFERENCES

American Express Spending and Saving Tracker, June 2010, Credit.com.

Assist News Service/Agape Press, 25/26 December.

Forbes Woman and the National Endowment for Financial Education (NEFE), online survey, credit.com.

http://healingprayer.wordpress.com/soul-ties/ Copyright © 1999–2008.

Lawyers.com.

Porn-Free.Org, http://www.porn-free.org/soul-ties.htm.

The Free Dictionary, www.thefreedictionary.com/ wholeness.

The National Endowment for Financial Education (NEFE), online survey, May 2011, credit.com.

*

CPSIA information can be obtained at www.ICGtesting.com
Printed in the USA
LVOW13s1530201213

366238LV00028B/866/P